The Angels' Little Diet Book

❀

The Angels' Little Diet Book

❁

HEAVENLY HINTS TO HELP YOU FIGHT FAT
BY EILEEN ELIAS FREEMAN

Pen-and-ink sketches by Leonard Day

Warner Books, Inc., 1271 Avenue of the Americas, New York, NY 10020

 A Time Warner Company

Printed in the United States of America
First Printing: May 1996
10 9 8 7 6 5 4 3 2 1

Library of Congress Cataloging-in-Publication Data
Freeman, Eileen E.
    The angels' little diet book : heavenly hints to help you fight
fat / Eileen Elias Freeman.
    p.   cm.
  ISBN 0-446-67212-2
  1. Weight loss. 2. Angels—Miscellanea. I. Title.
RM222.2.F725 1996
613.2'5—dc20   95-25570
                                         CIP

Many quotations from the scriptures have been taken from the New Revised Standard Version (abbreviated NRSV), copyright © 1989 by the Division of Christian Education of the National Council of the Churches of Christ in the United States of America and used by permission. Other quotations have been translated by the author and are indicated by the abbreviation EEE.

Book design by Eileen Elias Freeman   *Cover design by Julia Kushnirsky*
Artwork by Leonard Day   *Cover art by Paul E. Sheldon*

✠

To Leonard Day, my prayer partner,
my brother in Christ, and my dear friend,
whose support lifts my spirit to God and
brings me closer to Christ;
and to Gabriel Hart, a real angel,
who links us together in the Holy Spirit.

Contents

Preface

 $\mathcal{A}$ nyone who has ever read my earlier books *Touched by Angels* and *Angelic Healing*, in hardcover, will remember the picture of the author on the back flap—a photo of a woman clearly not in touch with her very fat body. But within the past two years, God has changed my life dramatically, and nowhere has the change manifested itself so much as in my body. Since April of 1994, I have lost more than 200 pounds, and I have lost them steadily, healthily, and with joy. I could never deny the massive effort involved, but the sense of spiritual support and confidence I received from God and from his angels has given me the certainty that I will not regain what

I have lost. I have learned some powerful lessons about how to lose unhealthy weight and how to keep it off. It has little to do with fancy diets, although obviously we must take in fewer calories than we need in order to burn off our stored fat.

It has to do with experiencing the love of the all-loving God for us, and realizing that God loves us, body and soul, and wants us to be healthy, happy, and joyful. It has to do with learning how our angels—the ancient and wise servants of God who minister to us—can help us live in the love of God. It has to do with loving ourselves and seeing ourselves through the eyes of God.

These lessons were some 47 years in coming to me. I've always learned academic lessons easily—the lessons of life have come much harder, probably because my weight was a wound even from my childhood.

Sometimes I think that the first word I ever learned to spell was "fat." The first dress size I remember as a child was called Chubbette. It was quickly followed by something called Junior

Plenty. By my teen years I learned that my fashion world was henceforth to be circumscribed by Lane Bryant (Fashions for Big Women) and the resourcefulness of my mother, an expert tailor.

At school, my spiritual pain began in fifth grade. A classmate named Mark began the taunts, the teasing, the insults. Other boys, eager to pal around with him, began to follow suit, until my life became a living hell of catcalls, mocking sounds whenever I came into the room, and even mild physical abuse. I was so withdrawn into my shell by the time I reached eighth grade that I never even reached the fringes of the adolescent parties, dating, cliques, and girl-talk that my classmates took such delight in. A gifted student, I took refuge in academic excellence—and in my faith in Christ, which gave me comfort.

But despite all my efforts and those of my parents, I grew fatter and fatter. Diets didn't work—they only filled me with fear and failure. It was the era of diet pills, which altered my personality without providing any lasting help. As each new effort failed, my self-esteem plunged further, until, even when I wouldn't admit it, I was filled with anger, despair, and a sense of my own worthlessness that made me hate myself.

I never dated—the memory of what Mark had done to me as a pre-teen made me too scared to seek out a boyfriend. Instead, I concentrated on scholastic success, and was rewarded with good grades, awards, scholarships.

But I was miserable on the deepest level of my badly wounded spirit. I felt isolated from others and from myself, and even from God. Oh, I never doubted that God loved me. After all, that was God's job, I believed. God *had* to love me—God didn't have a choice in the matter. But I was certain that God only loved my "soul." There was no way that God could love the whole me. I was too ugly, too much of a social failure, too fat.

In fact, I weighed 380 pounds at my highest weight. By the time I was in college I had knee problems. I lost my gall bladder to surgery, and later I developed cancer of the uterus, which was, praise

God, dealt with both surgically and through the help of God's angels (see my account in *Angelic Healing*, Warner Books, 1994). My blood pressure required medication, and my blood sugar was creeping up to unhealthy levels. All of these ailments were directly caused by or affected by my weight.

Added to this were the emotional wounds and scars, including decades of unhealed memories, deeply buried times when people turned away from me or abused me emotionally or rejected and made fun of me because of my weight. There were other painful memories—of different doctors' offices, of endless tests, of uppers and thyroid medications, of over-the-counter diet pills and starch blockers, and all sorts of nostrums that just didn't work.

In my whole adult life, I lost weight only twice, and each time required superhuman effort. On one of those occasions, a doctor gave me diet pills; on the other I drank a liquid protein—both times with medical supervision, of course. But through it all, I was filled with fear and anxiety that these efforts would fail. I had no energy left for anything except keeping to my diet. I became compulsive and controlling, rigid. It was the only way—or so I thought—to lose weight.

And I did lose weight—but at a terrible price to my spirit. In the end, I regained it all and more, because as my body shrank, so did my spirit. The secret to successful, permanent weight loss is to expand our spirits, not just to shrink our bodies. If we can learn to love, to trust, to give up all our fears into the hands of the loving God who cares so much about us, body, mind, and spirit, to lean on Christ, then we can lose all the weight we need, and we can do so in an atmosphere of joy, peace, and patience.

"There's nothing I can do about it—I was born to be fat!" some people have told me. And that might be true. There's no question in my mind that I have a genetic predisposition to obesity, as do other women in my family. I gain weight if I eat only 1,500 calories per day. I'm told I have a "cave woman" body type—one that saves up every calorie that comes its way and stores it so I'll survive the next Ice Age. And God loves me just as I am, right down to every additional fat cell.

However, the fact that my body can't handle food like most people's is no excuse to overeat. Yes, it's tough to realize that one can never eat like cousin Chris, who can eat a whole pizza at a time and never show an ounce. But that's the way it is right now. There are some promising studies on ways to permanently increase metabolism, and there are nutritional and exercise-related helps, but nothing has been shown to be *the* single answer to overweight, except for the most obvious and simplest (on paper!) answer: *Take in fewer calories than your body burns.*

So how did I finally "see the light"? Was there a revelation from heaven? Did my guardian angel Enniss appear before me holding a bunch of raw carrots in his hand?

Well no, not exactly. God very rarely rattles the thunder, unless there's no other way for us to get the message. But God always speaks to us in our hearts, and if we are very quiet, and we don't insist on interpreting things our own way, we can hear what the Spirit says.

One day back in March of 1994, I was simply working at my computer, proofreading the manuscript for *The Angels' Little Instruction Book,* and thinking how glad I was that there wouldn't be a picture of me in it. I wasn't trying to diet, because I knew it would be useless. And then, out of the blue, I heard these words from deep inside my soul: "Now is the acceptable time, now is the day of salvation." I recognized it as a quote from St. Paul's second letter to the Corinthians, and I knew, without knowing how, that God was calling me to lose weight once and for all.

"*I can't!*" I remember crying aloud. And I couldn't face the fear, especially the fear of failure, the disappointment, the struggle to lose weight that would last at least two years and the lifelong struggle to keep it off. It was overwhelming.

And then the Voice said, "I love you, my child. Let me help." The sensation of love that I felt made me cry. I didn't feel worthy of such love. All I could see were the years of fat and failure and deep self-hatred. "I can't!" I cried again.

"*But I can*," the Voice assured me. And the love rolled over me until I was quite breathless at its strength. I knew that this love was coming to me straight from the heart of Jesus, and after a time, I realized I believed the Voice.

"But how?" I asked. The task seemed too enormous even to consider.

"Don't be afraid." This was a different voice, and I recognized it at once as that of my own angel, whom God sends from time to time with His messages for my life. Each time, the angel has come when I have been afraid, and he has taken my fear away, because fear does not come from God but from the spiritual forces that would like to sift us like wheat.

At the angel's words (which really come from God, I believe), my fear lifted, and I felt a certain sense of peace and resolution and courage, and I knew, I *knew*, in a way I had never experienced before, that this indeed was the acceptable time, the day of salvation for me. I felt a great stillness and peace within, and a sense of being loved deeply and intimately by the greatest Lover the world has ever known. I asked for help, and then I said, "Now what do I do?"

And my angel, who is one of the ways in which God answers my prayers, said, "Sit back and let's talk. . . ." (Well, he didn't put it quite like that, of course, but I did sit back and start to listen to the Spirit.)

From April of 1994 to January of 1995 I worked hard at controlling my calorie intake. But just as important, I listened—to God, to my angels, to scientific wisdom on obesity, to the testimony of the word of God, to the language of my own body, and to the needs of my heart. The more I read the scriptures, the more I could see how they applied intimately to my struggle to lose weight and keep it off. I found that passages I had never associated with the subject kept coming to mind, and as I prayed about them, the little voice that had told me not to be afraid would explain how they related to my situation.

I had thought that my weight-loss regime would involve two years of torture, of relentless self-denial, of inner pain, of exhaustion (both mental and physical), of angst. I was wrong. *The only way to lose weight and keep it off is to love food deeply and to treat it as a wonderful, essential gift of a loving Creator.* And when you love someone, you listen to them, you pay attention, and you don't try to control or possess them. As I released my need to possess food, to control it, to play God with what I ate and didn't eat, many of my worst problems gradually went away, and as I gave my life more and more to Jesus, he gave me greater victory over still other problems. It's a victory for which I am still struggling in some areas, but I know now how to love food so much that I only eat the amount I need to be healthy. I know how to rejoice in the food I eat. I even know how to rejoice in food that I cannot eat any more (such as chocolate) or that I choose not to eat any more (such as meat).

I am now at a healthy weight for me, the least I've weighed since I was an adolescent. But I am not a fashion model. By current standards of beauty my body doesn't come close. It may, in time, but for me what is important is that by the grace of God I am now at a healthy weight, one that enables me to go anywhere and do anything I need to do in order to live within God's plan for my life.

The Angels' Little Diet Book does not contain a diet. What worked for me, in terms of what I ate and when, will not work for you. You must listen to your body and to the Spirit of God to know what you are supposed to do. Nor is it a book of angelic "whisperings" in my ear. I believe personally that God often works through his ministers and servants, the angels, and that he has done so in my case, but God may choose to speak to you in some other fashion. Trust me, God will speak to you, if you ask for help—through the Spirit, through others, through the Word.

The Angels' Little Diet Book is in three parts. The first is full of encouraging words from the scriptures and the deuterocanonical books, together with a short commentary as to how those scriptures affected my own walk with God. I suggest that you take one each day and reflect on the truth of God's word.

The affirmations are designed to be repeated several times a day, usually when you first get up, just before you turn off the light at night, and whenever you eat or drink, or on specific occasions. Affirmations aren't magic; they simply remind us of important truths we believe and attitudes we want to cultivate.

The blessings are, in a way, specialized affirmations that remind us that all foods are good and wonderful blessings from God, and that nothing is to be rejected if we can receive it with thanksgiving. Even if we choose to eat only one small forkful of our best friend's wedding cake, we should give no less fervent thanks for it than for an entire piece.

Let us pray for each other and thank God in advance for our success. God wants each of us to weigh whatever is most healthy for us, and that is not easy. Many forces exist that would like to sabotage our efforts, from well-meaning friends ("But I baked this pie especially for you!") to "spiritual forces of wickedness in high places." (Go ahead and pig out. You only live once.)

"But thanks be to God, who gives us the victory through our Lord Jesus Christ." (1 Corinthians 15:57)

Let me hear from you about how God has helped you become victorious over a weight problem. I'd like to spread the good news around. Write to me at the address below. God bless you!

Eileen Elias Freeman
The AngelWatch™ Foundation, Inc.
226 Robin Hood Road
Mountainside, NJ 07092
June 1995

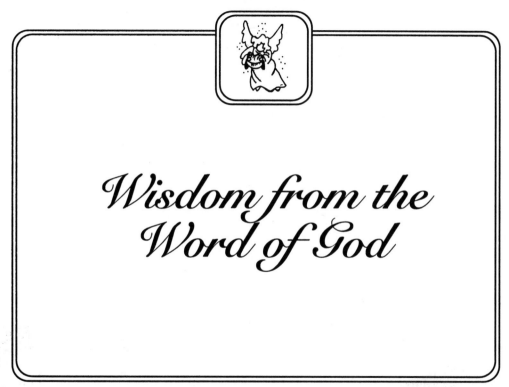

Wisdom from the Word of God

Many more scriptures deal with the love of God than with hate. Many more deal with rejoicing than with doom and gloom. If we want to lose weight and keep it off, we need to depend on God's laughter and God's joy, not on self-hatred and fear of punishment. The texts I have chosen from the canonical and deuterocanonical texts of scripture have helped me move ahead during many thousands of moments of trial and temptation. They have become old friends whose truth I know for myself. Prayerful reading of scripture, called *lectio divina* (divine reading), has nurtured many generations of seekers. The more you read, the more you can be blessed. The more you are blessed, the more you'll want to read, and the more God can change your life.

Now is the acceptable time;
see, now is the day of salvation!

—2 Corinthians 6:2 (NRSV)

❀

I'll start my diet tomorrow. How many times have we said that phrase, usually with a little guilt attached. Or worse, we start a program, then we overdo, and instead of picking ourselves up and asking God for more strength, we give in for the rest of the day and pig out. Now is the day of salvation! The only time we have at our disposal, to use for good or for ill, is Now! But the beauty of it is that we *always* have the Now. We can *always* step into the stream of Now and let it carry us toward our goal. No matter what your past was like, with the help of God, and the angels he sends to watch over us and bring us that help, you can succeed in losing weight and keeping it off. God loves every part of us, including our bodies, and God wants us to love our bodies, to nourish them, and to keep them in good condition.

I can do all things through [Christ] who strengthens me.

—*Philippians 4:3 (NRSV)*

❀

I don't believe that I could have lost a single pound and kept it off if I had not trusted in God for my strength every step of the way. I know, because I tried a dozen times, depending on my own willpower and inner strength. Each time I failed, because my own strength wasn't enough. But this time, I gave over to God all my weakness, relying on the almighty power of Christ, and I found that all the strength I needed was there. I just had to lean on God for help. Every day I still ask for help in knowing what I should and shouldn't eat, and in what quantity I should eat. And God, who knows my body much better than I, always sends my angels with the wisdom I need to keep on my program. Not only that, but God's angels rejoice with me. We're all happy—God, the angels, and I. I use the quote from Philippians as an affirmation every day, because it reminds me not only that my strength comes from God, but that I still have to do the work—even my angels won't take the french fries off my plate for me!

*Go, eat your bread with gladness,
and drink your wine with a
merry heart, for God has long ago
approved what you do.*

—Ecclesiastes 9:7 (NRSV)

❀

Why is it that we make eating such a source of anguish? God wants us to eat and drink whatever we need to make and keep us healthy. Every single food on the face of the earth is good in its own way, and unless we have an allergy or a medical condition that prevents us from enjoying something, we must not approach food with fear. Of course, we must be moderate, but only in how much we take. Our enjoyment, even if it's just of six potato chips or a small piece of angel food cake, should know no bounds. If we cultivate a merry heart at all times, we will find that we approach our meal times with joy and gratitude to God who has given us so much variety to delight our eyes, our nose, and our mouth. We won't feel deprived at all!

So, whether you eat or drink,
or whatever you do, do everything
for the glory of God.

—1 Corinthians 10:31 (NRSV)

❀

Oh, how I love this text! It reminds me that eating and drinking are positive values. Eating, even when we are limiting our food quite severely, is something we must do for the glory of God. Food is good, and has been ordained by God as the way we keep our bodies fueled. Eating is not meant to be a penance. We need to approach every meal, every snack with joy in our hearts, because to eat is to center ourselves in the divine plan for our lives. When we eat appropriately and not to excess (and "excess" will differ for each of us), we fulfill God's will. Sip your soda with joy, chomp your chicken with delight, pop your peas with panache, because a loving God has designed food to be a source of joy. Before you begin, ask that your whole eating experience give glory to the God who created food for our sustenance. It will change your attitude about broccoli!

No testing has overtaken you that is not common to everyone. God is faithful, and he will not let you be tested beyond your strength, but with the testing he will also provide the way out so that you may be able to endure it.

—1 Corinthians 10:13 (NRSV)

❀

How we deal with the ever-present temptation to go off our programs and cheat is what makes or breaks our weight loss. It's a terrible struggle, but remember that you're not alone. Testing is common to everyone. The perpetually slim neighbor you mistakenly envy may struggle just as much with temptations to go back to smoking or to throw herself off the bridge as you do with the urge to eat french fries. Reach out to a friend (and to our best friend, God) when you are sorely tested. In sharing is strength, because sharing gets us out of our private miseries and helps us see reality through more objective eyes.

My soul is satisfied as with a rich feast, and my mouth praises you with joyful lips when I think of you on my bed, and meditate on you in the watches of the night.

—Psalms 63:5-6 (NRSV)

❧

Virtually all our hunger is a hunger for God. St. Augustine once said, "You have made us for yourself, O God, and our hearts are restless until they rest in you." It's so easy when we are trying to lose weight to translate any need—whether for comfort, acceptance, or attention—into a need for food. But our physiological need for food is limited. Nearly every time we put something into our mouth and swallow it, it's because we *want* the food, not because we *need* it for the health of our bodies. One day when I prayed about this, God sent my angel to ask me to pray before putting anything in my mouth. I believe that if we ask God to show us whether our hunger is for food or for God, the Spirit will let us know. When I remember to do this, I never eat inappropriately.

*I have loved you with an
everlasting love; therefore I have
continued my faithfulness to you.*

—Jeremiah 31:3 (NRSV)

❋

Do you want to be successful at losing weight? Then learn to love. Fat is a prison that starves love or drives us to seek it in the wrong places and ways. We are wounded by times when people rejected us because of our physical appearance, and there comes a time when we believe we are less lovable than others. At that point we don't need others' rejection: we do it to ourselves at every possible opportunity! And finally, we not only put others at arm's length (do unto others before they do unto you!), we hold God away, too, believing that the loving Creator who placed us here hates us for being overweight. Wrong! Let me say that again. Wrong! God's love is all-encompassing and without conditions; God's faithfulness is everlasting. Reach out to love someone—a relative, a co-worker, a stranger—and you will feel less like eating. You'll already be "full."

Do not fear, for I am with you,
do not be afraid, for I am your God;
I will strengthen you, I will help you, I will
uphold you with my victorious right hand.

—Isaiah 41:10 (NRSV)

❀

The angels are always telling us not to be afraid. It's almost an axiom that an angelic message begins with the words "Fear not." But angels have no messages of their own. The words they bring to us come from God. It seems to me that God has been telling us not to be afraid for a very long time, and we still aren't listening. I know we can take the attitude that losing weight is something to make us nervous and afraid. But this is absolutely untrue. The best attitude we can have is a confident one, a loving one, a trusting one. The scriptures remind us that there is no room for fear in the loving heart, and that God, who is perfect love, has nothing fearful within. We are to imitate God, and that often means dealing with images of fear. God will help us.

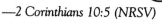

We take every thought captive to obey Christ.

—*2 Corinthians 10:5 (NRSV)*

❀

When I'm on a diet, my imagination often works overtime. I can visualize myself giving in to temptation at the party I'm going to be attending. I can see myself in my mind's eye having the pizza or the nachos or the buttered roll. I can already hear the well-meaning friend who will insist I try her spinach dip—at 300 calories a tablespoon! And even before I get where I'm going, I feel defeated. This happened to me many times, until one day I asked a very wise man, a priest, about this problem. He reminded me of the above scripture. "You don't have to deal with such thoughts," he explained. "You don't have to fight them, or think them through, or come up with alternate fantasies. Just take them captive." So now, when I see myself giving in at some hypothetical point in the future, I quickly take the incipient fantasy, put it into a mental garbage bag, and tie a knot in it. Or I put it down the garbage disposal and imagine Jesus flipping the switch to turn it on and grind the thought to rubble. It works for me.

The Angels' Little Diet Book / 11

No one, when tempted, should say,
"I am being tempted by God";
for God cannot be tempted by evil and he
himself tempts no one. But one is tempted by
one's own desire, being lured and enticed by it.

—James 1:13-14 (NRSV)

❀

Sometimes people joke about the huge piece of cheesecake they've just eaten by saying "The devil made me do it." Well, the good news is that the devil can't make you do anything you don't want to do. That's a promise from the Lord. So don't try to weasel out of the overindulging that can happen. Just because it's a retirement dinner for your pastor or a potluck supper to raise money for AIDS research, don't imagine that God will give you permission to stuff yourself! If you give in, well, tell God you're sorry, turn your face in the direction of the cross, get up again, and be happy for the strength of God that empowers the whole universe—and us, too.

I am confident of this, that the one who began a good work among you will bring it to completion by the day of Jesus Christ.

—Philippians 1:6 (NRSV)

❀

Purely human solutions will never work for all of us who constantly work to lose weight and keep it lost. This is because science and medicine simply do not have the perfect answer, especially for people with faulty metabolisms or wounds of spirit. Only the search for God and our willingness to place all our needs before him can provide us with the strength we need. But we can be sure of this: every diet that we begin in order to improve our health and enable us to serve God and each other with more energy and love is blessed already by God. God is the one who has begun this work in you, and God will bring it to completion if you trust in him and listen to his word to you.

Set a guard over my mouth, O Lord;
keep watch over the door of my lips.
—Psalms 141:3 (NRSV)

❀

Forgive me for taking this passage out of context to apply to those of us
fighting the battle of the bulge. In context it seems to refer to watching
what we say. But for me, the need for vigilance in my efforts to lose weight
and keep it off means that I have to be alert at all times. Who is the guard
that God will set over our mouths? For me, it has been my angel. I often
ask God to send that heavenly guard to keep me faithful to my program,
and he always does what God asks. Angels will not prevent you from
putting potato salad in your mouth and swallowing it, but they are
very good at reminding us how many calories are in a mayonnaise.
We can easily forget about the bagel we grabbed from the counter
as we ran out the door to work, but our angels never forget. They
can help keep us honest. Above all, ask them to pray for you,
as you would ask any of your human friends. Nothing makes
an angel happier than being asked to pray.

The Lord bless you and keep you;
the Lord make his face to shine upon
you, and be gracious to you; the Lord
lift up his countenance upon you,
and give you peace.

—Numbers 6:24-26 (NRSV)

❀

This passage has nothing in particular to say to dieters, but I include it because it is my prayer for you. I want you to know the light of God in your heart and on your face. I want you to know the peace of God that surpasses all our human understanding, but that provides the only groundwork for living in success. I pray that the blessing of God lightens your heart and gives you confidence in him. I ask him now to come into your life in a new way so you can experience in your own life the victory that comes to all through Jesus, the Son of God. Live in the light that comes from the face of God, and know how much he loves you.

Whatever is born of God
conquers the world. And this is the
victory that conquers the world,
our faith.

—1 John 5:4 (NRSV)

❦

Faith is critically important as we walk this world, particularly if we are trying to gain victory over a weight problem. But the faith that the scriptures speak of is not simply an "I think I can" kind of attitude. All we are, have, and do is intimately linked to the God who created us. Without faith in God, we are cut off from our very roots. How can we draw nourishment for our lives if we have no roots to feed us? Do things that build your faith in God. I particularly like reading prayerfully through the Acts of the Apostles, with all the wonderful things that happened because people placed their faith in God. Miracles happened, people were delivered from prisons, victories were gained at every turn in the road. Nurture your faith.

A little suffices for well-bred persons. When they lie down, they are not in discomfort.

—Sirach 31:19 (EEF)

❧

People who need to lose weight eat too much. It's a sad fact, but true. Overweight happens because we take in more calories than our body can burn, and so they are stored as fat. "But I eat like a bird, and I still gain weight!" you protest. That may well be true. No one ever said that I would need as many calories as the next person to maintain my weight. There comes a time when you have to accept the fact that your body doesn't need as many calories as all the books say you should be able to eat and not gain weight. "That's not fair!" I protested when it finally sunk into my brain. My angel replied, "What's unfair is stuffing your body with food it doesn't need. It's your wounded spirit that craves the food, not your body. If you give it just what it needs (not what your mind or your wounded ego wants) and no more, it will be happy." So I do—and it is.

*Distress and pain, loss of sleep
and restlessness are the lot of the
glutton! Moderate eating ensures a sound
night's sleep and a clear mind the next morning.*

—Sirach 31:20 (EEF)

❧

Have you ever seen those television documentaries on sharks, the ones where fish and blood are thrown in the water to attract these predators? First one or two sharks appear and nudge the food tentatively. Then more appear, until the water is full of aggressive sharks biting indiscriminantly at anything—even each other. A mindless feeding frenzy has taken over. Afterwards, the sharks go away and sleep it off. That used to happen to me regularly. Even when I had the table set with just the right amount of food for me, I would still take one look at it and start to bolt it, eating steadily, quickly, without even enjoying it! I would feel heavy afterward, and even fall asleep. Now I eat slowly, I breathe deeply, I enjoy my food, and I try to relax as I eat.

*God said, "See, I have given you
every plant yielding seed that is upon
the face of all the earth, and every tree with seed
in its fruit; you shall have them for food."*

—Genesis 1:29 (NRSV)

❧

According to the creation story in Genesis, the first people were vegetarians. It wasn't until after the Flood that God also gave Noah and his descendants permission to eat the animals. When I began my diet, I found that becoming a vegetarian helped me to stop obsessing about food, to eat more moderately, and to take pleasure in a wider variety of foods than I had ever known. I was able to eat more, because grains and vegetables are, in general, less calorie-dense than meats. I never thought I could be a vegetarian; I was raised in a "meat-and-potatoes" family. But when the angel of the Lord whispered to me one day as I prayed for help that I might be happier inside if my own nourishment didn't depend on the killing of animals, I tried it. It worked for me.

At mealtime Boaz said to Ruth,
"Come here, and eat some of this
bread, and dip your bread in the sauce." She sat
down beside the reapers, and he heaped up for
her some parched grain. She ate until she was
satisfied, and she had some left over.
—Ruth 2:14 (EEF)

❀

What a sensible text this is! We ought to eat at mealtimes, not only
because we are hungry then, but because mealtimes are social events
when we can be filled with the presence of other people and their
conversation, as well as with our food. Ruth was a sensible woman. She sat
down to eat; she didn't try to eat on the run. And she didn't eat until she
was stuffed—only until she was satisfied—and she had food left over.
Resist the temptation to clean your plate, if your body (or your angel) tells
you it has had enough. Save the leftovers or put them in the compost pile.

*Take delight in the Lord
and he will give you the desires
of your heart. Commit your way to the Lord;
trust in him and he will do this.*

—Psalm 36:4-5 (EEF)

❊

I started gaining too much weight as a child. My heart's desire—always frustrated—was to have a normal body. I prayed for it, I tried to work at it, and even when it seemed impossible, I still hoped for it. But it wasn't until I committed my diet, my hopes, and my whole life to God that it became possible. Why? Because I was trying to do everything myself. Food can become such an obsession in our lives that it is more powerful than we are; it can dominate us easily. But God is more powerful than anything else, including food. If we commit ourselves to the Lord daily, meal by meal, snack by snack, God will act, God will give us our heart's desire. "Let go and let God" is a popular saying. If we let God act, we will receive all the strength we need to eat only what we need and when we need it.

*The eyes of all look to you,
and you give them their food
in due season.*

—Psalm 145:15 (NRSV)

❀

How many times have we eaten when it wasn't appropriate? How many times have we gone to a party, stuffed ourselves, and then come home and fixed dinner, because it was dinner time, and we always eat dinner? Eating only "in due season" is one key to losing weight and keeping it off. When I began to lose weight, I asked God to send my angel to remind me about this, because I'm the sort of person who gets involved in her work and often forgets about eating at appropriate times. I learned to listen to my stomach, and to wait for it to tell me it needed nourishment, instead of listening to my mind and feelings. My feelings always wanted soothing and nourishing, because they'd been so wounded by rejection over the decades. I learned not to comfort them with food, but with the love of God, and by trying to love and help others in their need.

*If you are cheerful and gay
while at the table, you will benefit
from your food.*

—Sirach 30:25 (EEF)

❀

Diets can be scary. The very word *diet* contains the word *die*. We all know this. But I prefer to see "die" as in the phrase "The die is cast"; in other words, "I have made a decision, and I am going to stick to it." It's so important to have a positive and cheerful attitude to life. It makes everything, including losing weight and keeping it off, so much easier. When we sit down to our salad or our cottage cheese and fruit, it's easy to become so anxious about it that we never enjoy the taste; we may even make ourselves ill. We finish our food, not with gladness of heart, but with anxiety. Nutritionists tell us that fearful attitudes make it harder for our body to digest food and to absorb essential nutrients. Try to relax before you eat, giving thanks to God. Don't talk about food with your table companions or read negative books if you're alone. Cultivate cheerfulness.

The mouth can swallow any kind of food, but some foods taste better than others.

—Sirach 36:18 (EEF)

❊

I hate cottage cheese! And yet, when it came time to try yet another diet, I forced myself to eat it, because it was "good" for me, even though the texture of it made me almost sick. Mealtime would come, and I would be filled with anything but delight at the thought of sharing in God's creativity. Then God reminded me that in creating me as a unique being, I had legitimate preferences, even as far as food was concerned. Diets are not meant to be punishment! Make a list of all the things you like best to eat. Check off the ones you know are compatible with a weight-loss regimen. Put a star beside the ones you can eat little bits of just as they are. (You *can* learn to eat just one cookie.) Put a question mark beside the others and search for ways to make lower-calorie versions that you can eat, like pizza with low-fat cheese. Then enjoy the foods you like.

*Not every food is good
for every individual, nor is every
food suited to each taste.*

—Sirach 37:27 (EEF)

❀

Do you know how many diets there are? Thousands. There are grapefruit diets and banana diets, high-fat diets and low-fat diets, high-carb diets and low-carb diets. There are diets that ask you to eat a loaf of bread every day, and diets that suggest you eat lots of steak and lobster. That's because each of us is different, and our bodies react to food differently. Sometimes we have to try a variety of programs—or devise our own—before we find out what works for us. I found I couldn't lose weight when I ate meat, so I became a vegetarian. But my friend Kathy is allergic to dairy, wheat, corn, and soy, and she has lost weight eating lean poultry. Don't be afraid to try different approaches to weight loss. Remember that the first message of any angel is always "Don't be afraid." God loves you unconditionally, just as you are. You will find the combination or program that works.

Life is more than food.
—Luke 12:23a (NRSV)

❦

When we are struggling to lose weight, it is so easy to become obsessed with food. It fills our every thought. We dream of our next meal or snack. We fantasize about how we will prepare our salad, or which fat-free dressing we will use. We invent new seasonings for our skinless broiled chicken breast while we sort correspondence, or care for patients, or teach students. In other words, we make food our whole life at the very time when we should be making *Life* our life. Keep yourself distracted; stop thinking so much about food. Plan your day's meals ahead of time, so that when it's time to eat, you'll already know what you're going to eat. And then stop thinking about food. Dream instead of ways to save the earth, to help others, to improve your mind and expand your spirit. "Choose life," as God says in Deuteronomy 30:19. The more you think about others, the less power food will have over your life.

Jesus said to them,
"My food is to do the will of him
who sent me and to complete his work."
—John 4:34 (NRSV)

❀

Of all the things we do in the course of a day, food takes up a relatively small amount of time. We sleep, we work, we garden, we play golf, we jog, we sew, we write letters. The problem is that we often think of our daily routine as simply the activity that accompanies our eating or nibbling. For me, writing used to be what I did when I snacked. It got to the point where I couldn't even read a novel unless I had a certain food to eat at the same time! If we want to succeed in achieving and maintaining a suitable weight, we need to focus on identifying who we are and why we have been put here on earth. I believe we all have a purpose that no one else can accomplish. If our spirits are fueled by an understanding of what our earthly purpose is, then we can more easily fuel our bodies, without trying to make body-food a substitute for spirit-food.

For the kingdom of God is not food and drink but righteousness and peace and joy in the Holy Spirit.

—Romans 14:17 (NRSV)

❀

It's so easy for us to make food into a god, or at any rate, into something heavenly. Why else do we have angel food cake, divinity, heavenly hash, and other similarly named foods? (And strangely, they're usually high in calories and/or low in nutritional value, hardly a heavenly quality.) We need to feed ourselves with spiritual food and create heavenly recipes for nourishing our spiritual bodies. I have found that righteousness, peace, and joy are essential spiritual qualities to cultivate when we are working to lose weight. Righteousness, that is, acting rightly, with justice, helps us shed all sorts of guilt (and we often stuff ourselves when we feel guilty about something, don't we?). Peace frees us from anxiety (and how often do we eat when we're nervous?). Joy gets our minds off ourselves and into the stream of life around us, and we're too busy having fun to eat.

> *"All things are lawful for me,"*
> *but not all things are beneficial.*
> *"All things are lawful for me," but I will not*
> *be dominated by anything.*
>
> —1 Corinthians 6:12 (NRSV)

❈

We are free to eat anything we want to, and anything can be eaten in moderate amounts. But we must be prudent. I can eat a whole plateful of asparagus, or I can eat four or five macadamia nuts. God has given us every food on the face of the earth to eat, but if we are allergic to chocolate, then a candy bar will not be beneficial. If we want to succeed, we must not allow food to dominate us. We must stop being the prey of the potato chips on the supermarket shelf. We don't have to buy them, and if we have, we don't have to eat them. God put us on earth to have dominion over it, not to be slaves to it (or to destroy it through out aggression, either!). Say it to yourself when you have to deal with a food weakness: "With God's help I will *not* be dominated by *anything!*"

*Better is a dinner of vegetables
where love is than a fatted ox
and hatred with it.*

—*Proverbs 15:17 (NRSV)*

❀

One can lose—or gain—weight on both vegetarian and meat-eating diets. The author of Proverbs, following the custom of the day, was almost certainly a person who enjoyed meat, although a fatted ox was, even for the wealthy, holiday food. But isn't it true that, no matter what's being served, the attitude of the diners makes all the difference? I remember a family dinner where everyone was upset because some had arrived very late. There was no joy; the atmosphere was tense; and I just sat there and mindlessly shoveled food into my mouth. If we want to be successful, we need to make our tables places of calm, oases of peace and relaxation. Save for later all discussions of things about which you and others might disagree. If you're alone and watching the television, pick a show where the actors laugh instead of kill. Even your salad will taste better.

*Do not join those who drink
too much wine or who gorge
themselves on food.*

—Proverbs 23:20 (EEF)

❋

When I was a child I learned a prayer called the Act of Contrition. In it I promised God that not only would I try hard not to do hurtful things in the future but that I would also try to avoid the "near occasions of sin," that is, situations in which I was likely to give in to temptation. Losing weight can force us to make some hard choices, too. If we can't go into our favorite restaurant and order moderately, maybe we have to forget even going past it until we are stronger. If a good friend who likes to overindulge (or who can eat *anything* without gaining an ounce!) is a source of trouble to us, then maybe we have to find times other than meals to be with her or him. If we spend our time with people who eat inappropriately, we come to believe that such behavior is acceptable, or worse yet, that we can indulge in it ourselves. We can't.

Therefore, since we are surrounded
by so great a cloud of witnesses,
let us also lay aside every weight and the sin that
clings so closely, and let us run with perseverance
the race that is set before us . . .

—Hebrews 12:1 (NRSV)

❀

No matter what we do in our struggle to lose weight, we are not alone. We are surrounded by heavenly witnesses, both angels and human beings who have gone before us into the Kingdom of God. They all love us, and as they see us struggling, they pray for us, giving us friends in high places, indeed. Only we can run this race; it's hard and we must keep going. We must put aside sin and the burdens that weigh us down. Weight is death to an athlete in a race. God doesn't ask us to become fashion models, only to achieve a weight level that will enable us to run the race and live as God meant us to live.

> *. . . looking to Jesus, the pioneer and perfector of our faith, who for the joy that was set before him endured the cross, disregarding its shame, and who is now seated at the right hand of the throne of God.*
>
> —Hebrews 12:2 (NRSV)

❀

I once told someone that one of the secrets of losing weight and keeping it off was to live in joy. "How can you live in joy?" I was asked. "You're eating practically nothing, and you're fasting, and you're denying yourself all sorts of good food. How can you possibly be happy?" But I was, and I am, because I had a greater good in mind than a momentary palate-pleasing experience. With every mouthful I ate or didn't eat, I looked ahead in my mind to a new person, whose body would be healthier and happier, and the knowledge that the future would be wonderful gave me the strength to manage the present, as Jesus did.

"And whenever you fast, do not look dismal, like the hypocrites, for they disfigure their faces so as to show others that they are fasting. Truly I tell you, they have received their reward."

—Matthew 6:16 (NRSV)

❀

Misery loves company, an old saying reminds us. But I have found that in losing weight, one of the worst things I can do is to talk incessantly about my diet to everyone. Not only does it get boring, but we begin to hear all sorts of discouraging words from people who have tried half-heartedly and failed, and then we are filled with anxiety and fear. When we actually begin to lose weight, our friends will notice it and comment on it and even praise our efforts, but it's better to wait until they notice. Whether your personal program includes real fasting or not, try not to look like someone on a diet. Keep a smile on your face as you sip your goblet of seltzer!

Drink water from your own cistern,
flowing water from your own well.
—Proverbs 5:15 (NRSV)

❀

One of the most difficult situations for some who is trying to lose weight is to be invited out to dinner, or to stop for a quick bite at a fast-food restaurant. If someone invites you to their house, you worry about what they will serve, even if you've told them you're trying to lose some weight. If you're going out to eat, you worry whether the restaurant has something compatible with your regime. All told, dining out can be so nerve-racking that we fall into all kinds of traps. I've learned that it's easier to regretfully refuse dinner invitations when one is on a diet than to put oneself into situations that are hard to handle. I sometimes will accept an invitation, on condition that I bring my own food, or I suggest a restaurant that I know has something I can order and be happy about. I have even turned the tables around and invited people to my own house for dinner. Be careful about eating out, at least in the beginning. Real friends will understand and support you.

It is good not to eat meat or drink wine or do anything that makes your brother or sister stumble.

—Romans 14:21 (NRSV)

❀

Oh, how much there is to think about when we have told the world that we are working on losing weight! Not only do we actually have to demonstrate our shrinking waistline, but we have to be careful to set a good example for others. I remember going out to eat with friends who had been very supportive of my year-long efforts to lose weight. When I ordered a dish of pasta with a rather rich gravy, I could see in their faces that they were scandalized. After all, they had gone out of their way to encourage me, and had cooked special food for me when I was a guest in their house. I had to explain hastily that I had saved up every calorie I had for this one meal, and that I was only going to eat about 1,500 calories worth of the pasta. And that's what I did. So remember that other people are hoping with you and praying for you, and don't scare them!

Jesus said to [the disciples],
"Come and have breakfast."

—*John 21:12 (NRSV)*

❀

Almost every diet book will tell you that breakfast is the most important meal of the day. Our bodies need protein and some carbohydrates in order to get the inner furnaces stoked and working. When I skip breakfast, I feel very cold inside, as my body shuts down heat to the periphery in order to save it for the internal organs. I can deal with the cold by putting on more clothes, but the better way is to eat something that supplies protein. In the above case, Jesus had some bread and had also broiled some fish for his disciples. They had been fishing all night, and were exhausted. Fish might seem a bit unusual as a breakfast food, but there's no reason why you can't eat something different for breakfast. If you would rather eat a cold chicken leg for breakfast than some cottage cheese or an egg, why not? Remember that your body is unique, and what you eat is partly governed by your body's needs, your culture, and your preferences.

Remember that gluttony is evil.
No creature is greedier than the eye.

—Sirach 31:13 (NRSV)

❀

I have what's sometimes called a "cave-dweller body." It's very efficient at using energy and saves everything it doesn't need so that I will survive the next Ice Age. I start to gain weight after I eat about 1,500 calories a day.

That's not a lot of calories, but it's all I need. I can raise my limit a bit through vigorous exercise, but I don't have time for prolonged workouts.

When I eat far more than I know I need, it's gluttony or "pigging out." Gluttony is evil because in time it damages our body. It's also evil because it doesn't teach us anything about restraint. Our eye sees the cookies, or our nose smells the pepperoni pizza, and we conveniently forget that we just had a good meal or that we will be eating a little later. We need to set a limit to our eating, to go away from the table and count to ten, to walk around the block. Gluttony takes away from us our ability to remain in control of our eating. When you're tempted to pig out, step back from the food, and remember why you are trying to lose weight.

So when the woman saw that the tree was good for food, and that it was a delight to the eyes, and that the tree was to be desired to make one wise, she took of its fruit and ate; and she also gave some to her husband, who was with her, and he ate.

—Genesis 3:6 (NRSV)

❖

Well-meaning friends sometimes do us more harm than good, sabotaging our efforts with phrases like, "Just try one little piece. I made it specially for you. I even used *light* cream instead of heavy cream so it would be dietetic." Have a game plan, a set phrase that you can use in any circumstance to turn away such requests. If the one who offers is not someone you know well, a firm "No, thanks" together with a wave of the hand is usually enough. If it's a friend—or your mother—you may need to be more creative. Decline gently, but firmly, as often as you have to.

Jesus . . . returned from the Jordan and was led by the Spirit in the wilderness, where for forty days he was tempted by the devil. He ate nothing at all during those days, and when they were over, he was famished.

—Luke 4:1-2 (NRSV)

❈

Sometimes fasting is appropriate as a way of beginning, sustaining, or maintaining a weight loss. But unless you are fasting for just a few hours or a single day, it's essential to ask your doctor's advice. If you've never fasted before, always go to your doctor first. Jesus didn't eat for 40 days, and he was famished, as well as more subject to the blandishments of evil. I found fasting to be enormously helpful, and, with my doctor's approval, I fast two days a week on water. But what works for me might not work for you at all. However, if you can fast, know that the process not only helps you to hear the voice of God more clearly, but can help detoxify your body, too.

The tempter said to him, "If you are the Son of God, command these stones to become loaves of bread." But Jesus answered, "It is written, 'One does not live by bread alone, but by every word that comes from the mouth of God.'"

—Matthew 4:3-4 (NRSV)

❋

How Jesus deals with the tempter is a paradigm for all of us who struggle with the inner tempter that wants us to eat and eat and eat and hang the consequences. Have you ever had a craving, when you wished you could turn your low-fat cottage cheese into a sundae? Jesus reminded the devil that food is not the most important thing in life. I have found that one of the most effective ways to conquer the urge to eat what we shouldn't is to read the scriptures. I believe that in prayerful reading of the Bible we are in intimate contact with the Spirit of God, and that the Holy Spirit is infinitely more powerful than the voice of temptation.

Then the devil . . . placed [Jesus] on the pinnacle of the temple, saying to him, "If you are the Son of God, throw yourself down from here, for it is written, 'He will command his angels . . . to protect you.'" Jesus answered him, "It is said, 'Do not put the Lord your God to the test.'"

—Luke 4:9-10,12 (NRSV)

❀

I once did something that could have been very foolish. I was having a dreadful day. All I wanted to do was eat, and I kept daydreaming about everything from baked brie to chiles rellenos. Finally, I went to the nearest supermarket, took a deep breath, and said, "Dear God, I want everything in this supermarket, and I know it's all good, and if I wanted it, I could have it. But I'm not going to eat it, because I have a higher goal in mind." And I stood there, fighting the urges, crying out with pain. And God gave me victory. But it is better not to light backfires!

*Again, the devil took Jesus to a very
high mountain and showed him all
the kingdoms of the world . . . and he said, "All
these I will give you, if you will fall down and
worship me." Jesus said to him, "Away with
you, Satan! for it is written, 'Worship the Lord
your God, and serve only him.'" Then the devil
left, and suddenly angels came and waited on him.*

— Matthew 4:5-6 (NRSV)

❦

When we eat what we know we shouldn't, we make food into a kind of
Satan—a false god that can never bring us anything but disaster. But when
we turn our program over to God, angels are sent to minister to us, to help
us learn wisdom and to give us insight into what God's plan is for our lives.
We need to listen to God if we would hear the angels' voices.

The rabble among them had a strong craving; and the Israelites also wept again, and said, "If only we had meat to eat! We remember the fish we used to eat in Egypt for nothing, the cucumbers, the melons, the leeks, the onions, and the garlic."

—Numbers 11:4-6 (NRSV)

❀

Cravings! We are told that sometimes they represent the body's need for certain nutrients. But most of the time they represent simply our trying to satisfy a spiritual need with a physical food. The Israelites in the wilderness were well fed with manna, which supplied all their bodily needs, yet their inner dissatisfaction led to cravings. I'm not sure I ever craved garlic and cucumbers, but I have craved such things as smoked whitefish and gummy worms in my time. Identify your real craving, your inner spiritual need, before you decide to translate it into food for your body.

Speak to the Israelites and say to them: After you come into the land to which I am bringing you, whenever you eat of the bread of the land, you shall present a loaf as a donation [to the Lord].

—Numbers 15:18-20 (NRSV)

❀

Once, when I was praying, the Lord said to me, "Will you give me my tithe, Eileen?" I thought he meant 10% of my money, but as I prayed, I realized he also meant 10% of my time, my home—and my food. So nowadays when I put my food on my plate, I take a small portion (God is not a legalist!) and offer it to the Lord, quite literally. When the meal is over, I either set it outside for the wild creatures or put it in my compost pile, so it is not wasted. It reminds me that all my food comes from God, and helps me to be thankful. And when I go to the market, I always buy something for the needy and give it to the food bank at my church.

If you go into your neighbor's vineyard, you may eat your fill of grapes, as many as you wish, but you shall not put any in a container. If you go into your neighbor's standing grain, you may pluck the ears with your hand, but you shall not put a sickle to your neighbor's standing grain.

—Deuteronomy 23:24-25 (NRSV)

❀

I used to have a bad habit, whenever I went to a party or a reception, of hiding some food to take home with me. Once I stuffed my pocketbook with nuts and trail mix from bowls on the tables. How childish—as if I were afraid that God would not provide my food. If you are at a reception, try *not* walking around with a little plate. Take one piece at a time from the bowls or trays of food, and walk away to eat it before coming back for more.

Immediately Saul fell full length on the ground, filled with fear because of the words of Samuel; and there was no strength in him, for he had eaten nothing all day and all night.

—1 Samuel 28:20 (NRSV)

❀

God wants us to be strong and healthy during the whole time we are working on losing weight. This means that any time we do something foolish, like trying to starve ourselves, or forgetting to drink enough water, or just eating radishes, we run the risk of falling ill. Saul's collapse happened because, weakened by his depression, he forgot to eat, and the words of doom he heard were more than he could handle. We should never undertake prolonged or unusual regimens without competent medical advice. The human body is such a complex and marvelous creation of God that we cannot hope to know all about it ourselves.

"You are the salt of the earth; but if salt has lost its taste, how can its saltiness be restored? It is no longer good for anything, but is thrown out . . ."

—Matthew 5:13 (NRSV)

❦

Salt can be a real blessing to someone who is working on losing weight, or it can be a serious problem. Salt adds flavor to many foods, but in some people it can trigger problems with blood pressure. I used to eat with a fork in one hand and a saltshaker in the other. One day when I was praying, the Lord said, "Will you forego salting your food, Eileen? Will you be salt for other people's food instead?" In thinking about this request, I realized that my trying to be a source of spice and flavor for other people's lives was a way of taking my attention off my own food. I said Yes to God, and as soon as my taste buds had adjusted, I realized just how salty a typical American diet already is. I didn't need to add more.

Give us this day our daily bread.
—*Matthew* 6:11 *(NRSV)*

Give us each day our daily bread.
—*Luke* 11:3 *(NRSV)*

❧

When I was growing up, my family had a strange dinner ritual. Unlike most families, for whom dinner is the time to talk and share the day's activities, in my home we sat and ate silently, quickly, with total attention to the food. Once dinner was over, however, we began to talk and share just like most families. One day I asked my parents why we ate dinner like that. After thinking it over, my father said, "You know, chicken" (he always called me that!) "when I was a boy we never had much, because we were so poor. If you talked instead of eating, someone else got the leftover potatoes!" The habit of hunger persisted all his life, even though by the time I was born my father was earning a good living for his family. He never quite learned to trust that God would give him each day the food he needed. Learn to trust that God knows the measure of food your body needs, and that it will be there for you.

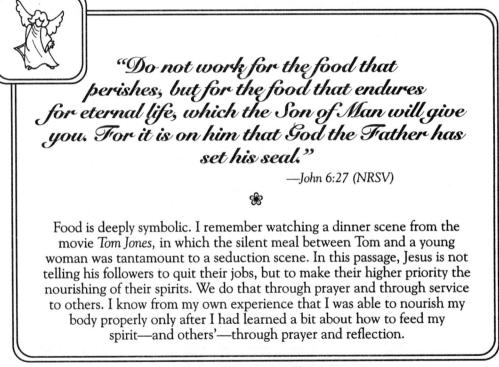

"Do not work for the food that
perishes, but for the food that endures
for eternal life, which the Son of Man will give
you. For it is on him that God the Father has
set his seal."

—John 6:27 (NRSV)

❀

Food is deeply symbolic. I remember watching a dinner scene from the
movie *Tom Jones*, in which the silent meal between Tom and a young
woman was tantamount to a seduction scene. In this passage, Jesus is not
telling his followers to quit their jobs, but to make their higher priority the
nourishing of their spirits. We do that through prayer and through service
to others. I know from my own experience that I was able to nourish my
body properly only after I had learned a bit about how to feed my
spirit—and others'—through prayer and reflection.

*All fat is the Lord's. It shall be
a perpetual statute throughout
your generations, in all your settlements:
you must not eat any fat or any blood.*
—Leviticus 3:16b-17 (NRSV)

❦

Yes, I know I'm taking this verse a bit out of context, but bear with me. Let's face it, we all eat too much fat. Why? Fatty food is more delicious than nonfat food, because the mouth feel is richer. Given a choice, most people will take ice cream over ice milk any day. In Bible days, the fatty portions of every slaughtered animal were to be burned by the priest as an offering to the Lord. I think we need to make this kind of offering, in a spiritual sense, ourselves. When we cut off the nice, crispy chicken skin, when we don't put the bacon bits on our salad, when we choose the fat-free dressing, let us do it as a free-will offering to God, and turn the occasion into a time of prayer, asking our angels to take our sacrifice to God's altar in heaven, so to say, and bespeak the grace we need to continue on our programs.

Now Eglon the King of Moab was a very fat man. . . .

—*Judges 3:17 (NRSV)*

❀

Talk about calling a spade a spade! Every language has its euphemisms to describe people who carry around more weight than they should. I heard it all as a child. I wasn't fat, I was "pleasingly plump." But there was nothing pleasing about it to anyone. Nowadays in the "personal" ads, one can read, "Rubenesque SPW seeks statuesque SPM for friendship and walks on the beach," etc. We all know what that means. It's a dodge, a way to avoid reality. The truth is that we weigh too much. And that can be painful to acknowledge, even when the weight came on us in our youth before we realized the whys and hows. But the good news is that truth is a godly thing, and where the Spirit of God is, there also is freedom. If we can call our weight what it is, honestly and simply, without self-condemnation, we have won half the battle. Living in truth and reality empowers us to take the steps we need to lose weight and keep it off.

Some believe in eating anything,
while the weak eat only vegetables.
Those who eat must not despise those who
abstain, and those who abstain must not pass
judgment on those who eat; for God has
welcomed them.

—Romans 14:2-3 (NRSV)

❋

No, this passage doesn't mean that vegetarians are inherently weak. Paul is
talking about people who pass up the meat course at dinner for reasons
pertaining to religious law. But how often do you secretly criticize an
overweight friend who reaches for dessert or a pat of butter? "Doesn't she
know how many calories there are in mayonnaise?" you think. "He
shouldn't eat so many cookies." Or perhaps you've been criticized for
having some special food for which you've saved calories all day. Put on
compassion, and give up judging. It's a happier way to live.

*Those who eat, eat in honor
of the Lord, since they give thanks
to God; while those who abstain, abstain in
honor of the Lord and give thanks to God.*

—Romans 14:6 (NRSV)

❀

I believe that anything we put in our mouths should be preceded and followed by giving thanks to God. And I believe that when we choose not to eat something, because either it's the wrong time to eat or the wrong kind of food for the moment, we should also give thanks to God. Grace before and after meals is an ancient tradition. Unfortunately, in today's world we often eat quickly and mindlessly, stoking our bodies whether they need it or not. Grace and thanksgiving remind us that we are intimately tied into a loving God, body, mind, and spirit, and that this God has provided us with the food we eat and the water we drink.

If your brother or sister is being injured by what you eat, you are no longer walking in love. Do not let what you eat cause the ruin of one for whom Christ died.

—Romans 14:15 (NRSV)

❀

The minute we begin to succeed in losing weight, friends and relatives start to offer their congratulations. And there's no doubt that those who love us, and who have seen us struggle, win, fail, struggle again and again, want us to win once and for all. Sometimes they take an almost proprietary interest in our success. After I first spoke about my weight loss in *AngelWatch*, the magazine about angels that I write, I found I had a host of new supporters who pray for me and who might be scandalized if I really pigged out. Every time I'm tempted to overdo a meal or a snack, I think of how they would feel if they saw me, and it reminds me that I have a responsibility to those who love me to work hard and trust God for strength to succeed.

Do not, for the sake of food, destroy the work of God.

—*Romans 14:20 (NRSV)*

❦

We are the "work of God," according to Paul, a wonderful, glorious work, unique, holy, precious, beloved, destined for eternity, not just this world. But what happens to our spirits is partly determined by how we treat the space suits in which they live while we are here on earth. It is certainly possible for food—either too much or too little—to destroy us. We all know of eating disorders like bulimia and anorexia. We may have had to deal with such conditions ourselves. But we are not going to fall into one extreme or the other, because our God wants us to steer a moderate course. Whenever I am tempted to overdo, when I reach for another yogurt or another piece of bread I don't need, I often stop myself, change my thoughts, and offer a prayer for all those who have to deal with clinical eating disorders, asking God to heal the inner wounds and hurt memories that can trigger such disorders. I send my angel to give them a hug for me, and usually when I finish, the urge to eat inappropriately is gone.

If God is for us, who is against us?
He who did not withhold his own Son,
but gave him up for all of us, will he not with him
also give us everything else?

—Romans 8:31-32 (NRSV)

❦

Sometimes the prospect of a long program to lose weight, together with the realization that "eternal vigilance is the price of liberty" can be so daunting that we almost despair even before we begin our diet. But as much as you want and need to lose weight, even more is the Creator of all things behind you. In fact, know that God is the one who has inspired you to want to achieve a healthier weight. God has given us everything. Surely God, who has given us the courage and love for ourselves to want to lose weight, will give us the strength to do so. We have the daily help of our angels, who always want what God wants. They can remind us of everything from the need to say grace to the number of potato chips we have mindlessly crunched at a party. Rejoice! We have friends in high places!

*For You love all things that exist,
and hate nothing that You have
created; for if You had hated something, You
would not have created it in the first place.*

—Wisdom 11:24 (EEF)

❀

Make no mistake about it—our bodies are wonderful creations of God. It doesn't matter whether your body is perfect by some artificial standard—God loves your body just as it is. You don't have to slim down and muscle up to an insurance company idea of "normal" for God to love your body. But love means much more than a warm, fuzzy feeling. It means taking a personal interest in helping another (or ourselves) achieve true happiness. God is that way for you. The One who made your body is not a nagging parent who threatens you with every glass of milk that isn't skim! God embraces you, body and soul, with supportive love and caring, and in God's name, so do the angels who watch over you.

*I appeal to you therefore,
brothers and sisters, by the mercies
of God, to present your bodies as a living
sacrifice, holy and acceptable to God, which is
your spiritual worship.*

—Romans 12:1 (NRSV)

❀

How can presenting our bodies to God be spiritual worship? At one point in my life, I found certain philosophies attractive. They emphasized transcending the body, its desires, its wants and hungers. They suggested that the body, when compared to the spirit, is somehow not just secondary, but even wicked. Because I hated my body and myself for being fat, I found these ideas consoling for a short while. But the more I tried to forget I even had a body, and to live as an impossibly "spiritual" creature, the more enmeshed in depression I found myself. We must realize that our bodies are holy and altogether suitable as an offering to God.

*Now the Lord is the Spirit,
and where the Spirit of the Lord is,
there is freedom.*

—2 Corinthians 3:16-17 (NRSV)

❦

Being overweight, particularly if we have been that way for a long while, is like living in bondage. In extreme cases, the extra weight can constitute a physical handicap, limiting what we can do, where we can go, what we can enjoy. Example: How do you travel a long distance—or even go to the movies—if you can't fit into the seat? But physical freedom is only part of the issue. Often the bondage is a spiritual one, due to years of low self-image. Angels are spirits, but they are not fairy godmothers who wave magic wands and give us favors. If we want our inner spirit to be free, so that our outer body can follow suit, we must turn to the supreme Spirit, the Holy Spirit of the Lord, who can heal the wounds inside that have prevented us from losing weight and keeping it off.

*Do you not know that you are
God's temple and that God's Spirit
dwells in you? If anyone destroys God's temple,
God will destroy that person. For God's temple
is holy, and you are that temple.*

—1 Corinthians 3:16-17 (NRSV)

❀

The scriptures use a number of metaphors to describe the way our spiritual
body relates to our physical body. The latter is called a temple, a tent, or a
dwelling. The Temple of God in Jerusalem was the holiest place on earth
to the Jews. We need to recapture a sense of just how holy our bodies are,
so that we can cease mistreating them and instead treat them with
reverence. I find that worshiping in church with others helps me see this
clearly, because a house of worship is never holier than when it is filled
with people praying together. At such times I try to identify myself with
the "temple," and I worship the living God who dwells within me.

Food will not bring us close to God.
We are no worse off if we do not eat,
and no better off if we do.

—1 Corinthians 8:8 (NRSV)

❀

Paul is speaking here of eating particular foods, not of eating or not eating. He is reminding his listeners that neither steak nor beans nor celery nor General Tso's chicken is inherently holy or intrinsically evil. We need to remember that. It's not a good idea to keep ourselves from eating pizza, for example, by thinking, "Pizza is terrible. It's full of cholesterol and calories and fat." Pizza is not a terrible food at all, if we eat it wisely. Somehow inside we are afraid that if we eat one piece of pizza, we will not stop there, so we dump every fear-filled, negative notion we can upon the innocent food that is our weak spot. Try to face food honestly and without fear. The angels remind us not to be afraid—not even of food.

*Stay awake and pray that you
may not come into the time of trial;
the spirit indeed is willing,
but the flesh is weak.*

—Matthew 26:41 (NRSV)

❀

The only way I have been able to succeed in losing weight joyfully and
keeping it off is through prayer. I say it frankly, with totally assurance that
I'm right on. When we approach weight loss, a healthier body, a new
lifestyle, we are, in fact, seeking healing for our lives, and I believe that
healing comes from God, who pours it out abundantly on us if we but ask.
And I think we need to put as much energy into our prayers as we can.
Jesus even urged his disciples to stay awake to pray. We have to put our
hearts into prayer, our energies, our strength, not as if it all depended on
us, or as if our energies can force some concession from God, but because
the measure of the energy we pour into our prayer is the measure of how
much we expect to succeed, by the grace of God.

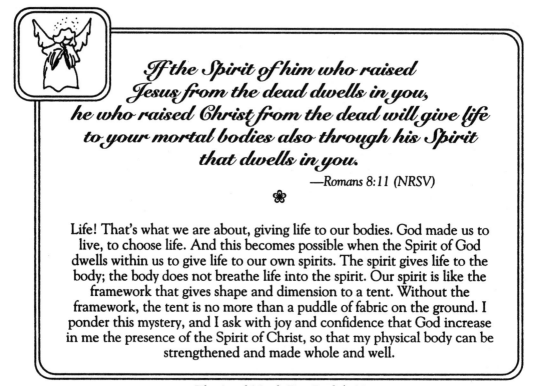

*If the Spirit of him who raised
Jesus from the dead dwells in you,
he who raised Christ from the dead will give life
to your mortal bodies also through his Spirit
that dwells in you.*

—Romans 8:11 (NRSV)

❀

Life! That's what we are about, giving life to our bodies. God made us to live, to choose life. And this becomes possible when the Spirit of God dwells within us to give life to our own spirits. The spirit gives life to the body; the body does not breathe life into the spirit. Our spirit is like the framework that gives shape and dimension to a tent. Without the framework, the tent is no more than a puddle of fabric on the ground. I ponder this mystery, and I ask with joy and confidence that God increase in me the presence of the Spirit of Christ, so that my physical body can be strengthened and made whole and well.

No treasure is greater than a healthy body; no happiness is better than a merry heart!

—Sirach 30:16 (EEF)

❀

Contemporary culture has produced an image of the so-called perfect body that is virtually unattainable, because God never intended for us all to look the same. I will never weigh 125 pounds wringing wet; I feel healthy and happy at a higher weight. We can make ourselves unhappy and sick by looking at a chart that arbitrarily decides what we should weigh, and setting our sights on that goal. We need to listen to God and to our bodies, because the goal of any diet or other program is to produce a healthy body. And when we have achieved or are well on the road to achieving that goal, we are happy and our hearts are merry. Keep the goal of health in mind rather than a new waist size. Health is a spiritual quality as well as a physical one, while a clothing size is a mark on a tape measure.

*So I find it to be a law that when
I want to do what is good, evil lies
close at hand. For I delight in the law of God in
my inmost self; but I see in my members another
law at war with the law of my mind, making me
captive to the law of sin that dwells in my members.*

—Romans 7:21-23 (NRSV)

❀

Make no mistake about it: taking back our health is a project that makes
certain spiritual powers of evil very unhappy! If you don't believe that
destructive spirits exist and would like to sabotage your efforts to achieve
lasting health of body (and soul, of course), then look around you, or, as
Paul reminds us, look within you. The bad news is that these fallen spirits
will try to derail your train. The good news is that the Spirit of God is
infinitely more powerful than these spirits, and loves us infinitely, too. By
trusting in God, not in our own power, we can stay on track and succeed!

Once when Jacob was cooking a stew, Esau came in from the field. He said to Jacob, "Let me have some of that stew; I'm starving!" Jacob said, "First sell me your birthright." . . . So Esau sold his birthright to Jacob—and ate the lentil stew.

—Genesis 25:29-31, 33 (EEF)

❀

It's amazing the power that food can have in our lives! Here is Esau, son of a wealthy sheik, not a man to live in want, who comes in from the field so hungry that he sells his birthright for some lentil stew. How often do we let a little emptiness in our stomach rule us? We come in late from work, and while we make dinner we're snacking on anything we can find, figuring we'll subtract the calories from what we eat at dinner. And do we? Not as a rule. Never eat standing up. If you took it from the fridge or cupboard, first put it on a plate, then on the table, then sit down to eat it. Don't rush.

Manoah said to the angel of the Lord, "Allow us to detain you, and prepare a kid for you." The angel of the Lord said to Manoah, "If you detain me, I will not eat your food; but if you want to prepare a burnt offering, then offer it to the Lord."

—Judges 13:15-16 (NRSV)

❀

Find loving and creative ways to overcome the efforts of people who may try to sabotage your diet with food. Parents and spouses can do this out of love. If we—or they—have used food in the past as a comfort for example, our loved ones, not understanding we are trying to change our attitudes about food, may offer us our favorite snack. Or at the dinner table, we may be pressed to have an unneeded second helping. The angel who came to Manoah and his wife was quite firm. So must we. In your heart, offer your meal to the Lord. Ask your angel to help you be loving—and to say No.

> *"Blessed are you who are hungry*
> *now, for you will be filled."*
> —Luke 6:21 (NRSV)

❀

Jesus is talking here not just about physical hunger, but about being filled
with God in this world and the world to come. For me, this passage is also
about deferring our wants and desires in favor of a better goal. Sometimes,
when I am hungry and trying to stare down some free cheese samples in
the specialty store I patronize, or when I want to order sesame noodles at
my local Chinese restaurant, but don't have any more calories in my daily
budget, I think to myself: "You can have those noodles any time you want,
dear heart. You are free, not in bondage. If you want those noodles, go
ahead and eat them." And then I think of my goal—to have as healthy
and happy a body as I can, so I can do all the things God has in mind for
me to do—and I say, "Yes, I know I am free to eat these noodles, and I
will—*but not today.* For today, I choose to eat something else. I decide to
defer my enjoyment to a more appropriate time."

"But woe to you who are full now, for you will be hungry."

—Luke 6:25 (NRSV)

❀

Why are we so afraid of hunger? The fact is that few people reading this book will have ever known hunger. Oh, yes, we've all had stomachs that growled when we were late for lunch. But that's not hunger. I find that when I fast for a few days, all sensation of hungriness goes away totally after a day or two. Real hunger is the body's protest when we have used up all our reserves, and yet no food is forthcoming. Real hunger is a danger signal. Real hunger is the fuel gage on empty. So why are we afraid of a little emptiness in our stomachs, unless it's a reminder of some ache, some emptiness in our souls that we haven't come to grips with? We need to let ourselves experience a little hungriness regularly. First of all, it reminds us that we need food to live. Second, it reminds us that just as our bodies hunger for food, so our spirits hunger for God. Third, it enables us to talk to our bodies, to be more in touch with them. It helps open the lines of communication with our bodies so we can understand their needs.

Is not this the fast that I choose:
to ... share your bread with the hungry,
and bring the homeless poor into your house ...

—Isaiah 58:6-7 (NRSV)

❦

Fasting has been an important part of my program since I began. I make a distinction between fasting for spiritual reasons, and fasting to cleanse the body. I do not fast in order to lose weight, but to make myself one with the hungry, and with the Lord who fasted for 40 days in order to seek God's will for his ministry. However, fasting, even for spiritual reasons, has the benefit of giving my mind a respite from having to think about food. If you can fast, ask God if you should do so periodically, and seek competent medical advice about how to do it. Then follow the advice in Isaiah, so that fasting doesn't become an egotistical trap. Consider what you would have spent on food during the days you decide to fast, and give the money or an equivalent amount of food to an organization that helps feed the hungry. Or better, yet, join the organization, and serve them yourself.

Jesus said to them, "I am the bread of life. Whoever comes to me will never be hungry, and whoever believes in me will never be thirsty."

—John 6:58 (NRSV)

❀

More than anything else I have done or tried to do, trusting in God has helped me to lose weight and to know how to keep it off. I don't trust in angels, as if they were independent fairy godmothers who wave magic wands over me; but I do trust in the God who sends them to protect me and to inspire me and even to warn me. The real food is the food that sustains our spirits. If we nourish our souls properly, generously, and often, it becomes much easier to nourish our bodies without going overboard. When we put God first, and not our bodies, then the truth of Jesus' words becomes evident in our lives.

*God has not given us a spirit
of cowardice, but instead a spirit
of power and of love and of self-control.*

—2 Timothy 1:7 (EEF)

❉

When I began my new lifestyle, I looked ahead—and was so scared I
almost gave up before I started. I thought about days, months, years, of
new eating habits, of foods I would need to restrict in favor of higher goals,
and at first I thought, "I can't do it." But this scripture came to mind, and
as I prayed about it, I realized that I not only needed new external habits,
but I needed new spiritual habits of courage. God gives us—in our every
need—power, love, and self-control. Power in this sense is not the power
of the world, but of the Spirit, internal fortitude and strength to accomplish
our goals. Love is the climate in which we achieve our goals. We must
work to lose weight and keep it off and build a healthy lifestyle our of love
for ourselves. Self-control is the great tool that the Spirit gives us to use,
and if we simply ask God for these gifts, they are ours in Jesus the Lord.

*For this very reason, you must
make every effort to support your
faith with goodness, and goodness with
knowledge, and knowledge with self-control,
and self-control with endurance, and endurance
with godliness, and godliness with mutual
affection, and mutual affection with love.*

—2 Peter 1:5-7 (NRSV)

❀

Just because we know all about dieting, about eating sensibly, about
nutrition and exercise doesn't mean that we put what we know into
practice. Losing weight and keeping it off is not so much a balance as the
growth of an inner structure whose elements build on each other. Faith is
the foundation, but notice that self-control and endurance are just as
much a part of the building as affection and goodness. Make every effort!

Now, discipline always seems painful rather than pleasant at the time, but later it yields the peaceful fruit of righteousness to those who have been trained by it.

—Hebrews 12:11 (NRSV)

❀

We all know about how painful it is to discipline ourselves to keep to a program that may include food restrictions, regular exercise, prayer, sharing with others, inspirational reading, and more. It's painful, partly because the little baby inside us still focuses on its own wants and screams for attention and nurturing, and partly because external forces for evil make things harder than they are. The key lies in nurturing ourselves through means other than food and drink. When a baby cries for no apparent reason, a mother will cuddle the infant or distract it with a rattle. When the discipline of dieting becomes painful, try to cuddle yourself and let God hold you in the arms of love. And remember to distract yourself with something pleasant—you'll know what that is better than anyone else.

> *"For John came neither eating nor drinking, and they say, 'He has a demon'; the Son of Man came eating and drinking, and they say, 'Look, a glutton and a drunkard, a friend of tax collectors and sinners!' Yet wisdom is vindicated by her deeds."*
>
> —Matthew 11:18-19 (NRSV)

❀

It's amazing how sometimes it seems you can't please anyone. So, as the old rock-and-roll song goes, "You have to please yourself." Do what you know to be true and right for yourself and don't let others sway you with criticism or even with name-calling. If being very restrictive in your food and drink, if fasting seems good to you, then with proper guidance you should go for it. If you feel better eating gourmet foods that fit within your calorie and nutrition budgets, then do it. I've tried both at different periods, and both were helpful. God is the God of all foods on earth.

> *"Ask, and it will be given you; search, and you will find; knock, and the door will be opened for you. For everyone who asks receives, everyone who searches finds, and for everyone who knocks, the door will be opened."*
>
> —Matthew 7:7-8 (NRSV)

❀

The promises of God may well have conditions on them, but they are loving conditions. Sometimes the process is like a game, in which one step provides instructions on getting to the next step. So if I "ask" God for a healthy, slimmer body, God's instructions to me are to "search" to find it. The searching can be long and involved, and when I find my new body, I still have to "knock" on the door. Sometimes we have to keep on knocking. God never said he would answer the doorbell on the first ring. Sometimes we need to keep knocking to realize just how much we either want or don't want our cherished goal.

*"So do not worry about tomorrow,
for tomorrow will bring worries of
its own. Today's trouble is enough for today."*
—Matthew 6:34 (NRSV)

❄

When I first began my own program of weight loss and a new lifestyle, I realized that it would take nearly two years just to reach my goal. And on some days, the temptation was to see the weeks and months of hard work, carrot sticks, and walks around the block that still lay ahead. I found that when I did this, I began to fear and to doubt my ability to succeed. But this scripture came to mind, and I realized just how important it is for anyone struggling to emerge into the sunlight. We must keep our end in sight, but we need smaller goals even more. My goal is to eat what I need to eat—today. To exercise—today. To pray—today. Don't borrow from tomorrow problems that might never come. Focus instead on the present, where God's love and grace and the help of the angels are always present to us. One step at a time can take you on a walk around the world.

*I praise you, for I am fearfully
and wonderfully made. Wonderful are
your works; that I know very well.*

—Psalms 139:14 (NRSV)

❧

When we live with fat for a long time, our self-image often becomes
warped. We look at ourselves in the mirror and we think all sorts of ugly
things that I won't even dignify by repeating here. I believe it is wrong of
us to do this. Our bodies are creations of God. The life in them is
inherently holy and blessed, because it proceeds from God. The divine
light is already bursting out from every cell. We need to give thanks to
God every day for our bodies, even if we still have enough "body" for
two! God gave us our bodies as an act of love, and it defeats the power
of God's love if we view our bodies as intrinsically evil or bad or sinful.
Your body is inherent sacred, because God, who created it, is holy.

For we do not have a high priest who is unable to sympathize with our weaknesses, but we have one who in every respect has been tested as we are, yet without sin. Let us therefore approach the throne of grace with boldness, so that we may receive mercy and find grace to help in time of need.

—Hebrews 4:15-16 (NRSV)

❀

God understands everything we're going through in our struggles to lose weight and keep it off forever. God understands, because God took a human nature in the person of Jesus, and Jesus went through everything we go through. The difference is that Jesus was perfectly victorious. If we trust in him and ask his help, we shall be victorious, too. But we must ask, we must approach the throne of grace.

Many live as enemies of the cross of Christ.... Their end is destruction; their god is the belly; and their glory is in their shame; their minds are set on earthly things.

—Philippians 3:18-19 (NRSV)

❀

"Their god is the belly." Paul has no compunctions about calling a spade a spade! Of course he is talking about more than just overeating; he is speaking to those who pursue their own selfish goals to the exclusion of all else. But whenever we listen only to the voice of our stomach, and when we give our body more food than it needs or wants, then we are falling into the trap Paul warns about. Taken to extremes, indulging in a passion for ice cream or sushi or even fat-free cookies can be tantamount to idolatry, especially if food blinds us to the needs of others. The good news is that we can achieve our earthly goal if we will set our minds on heavenly goals and let our spirits lead our bodies.

But our citizenship is in heaven;
it is from there that we are expecting
a Savior, the Lord Jesus Christ. He will
transform the body of our humiliation that it may
be conformed to the body of his glory, by the
power that also enables him to make all things
subject to himself.

—*Philippians 3:20-21 (NRSV)*

❀

These verses continue the thought of the text on the previous page. Paul speaks of victory for those who keep their aspirations high. Our bodies can and will be transformed, if we make the necessary effort. But we must remember that it is not by our own power that this will happen, but by the power of Christ, in whose hands is all power in heaven, on earth, and everywhere else. Believe me, that's enough power for any dieter!

*Do not fear, for I am with you,
do not be afraid, for I am your God;
I will strengthen you, I will help you, I will
uphold you with my victorious right hand.*

—Isaiah 41:10 (NRSV)

❀

Someone once said, "Work as if everything depended on you; pray
as if everything depended on God." It's a popular saying, but it's not
scriptural, and I think it's a mistake. God not only upholds our prayer,
God supports our work as well. God tells us plainly, "I will help you." So
why do we try to diet alone? I once thought that because my past eating
habits were so full of self-indulgence, I couldn't ask God to help me
lose weight, since it was my fault I'd gained it. I could only ask God
to help me keep it off once I had struggled to lose it. Wrong! God is
eager to help us to get rid of weight we don't need to carry. Just ask
for help. It's already there waiting, even before you can ask.

God is in the midst of her;
she shall not be moved;
God will help her at the break of day.

—Psalms 46:5 (?)

❋

I'm not sure what translation this psalm verse is taken from. It was given to me orally over the telephone one day. I had been struggling against the urge to eat everything in sight and was so tired I wanted to die! I was actually discouraged on some spiritual fronts, and the need to assuage my spiritual angst with food was the result. We all do it from time to time, as illogical as it is when you think about it. Then my prayer partner and dear friend Leonard called me to say that in prayer, God had sent the angel Gabriel to him with a message for me: "Tell Eileen to take comfort in Psalm 46:5." Leonard had checked the reference out and had called me immediately to share it. I was so grateful for God's loving reassurance that the gloomy mood was broken at once. God will give us the victory, for God is in our midst. We shall not be moved.

Rejoice in the Lord always;
again I will say, Rejoice.

—Philippians 4:4 (NRSV)

❋

About midway through my weight-loss program, I found myself in the middle of the Christmas season and a frantic schedule of talks, classes, workshops, media appearances, and parties. I give more talks about angels during the holidays than at any other time of the year, and my schedule was hectic. I began to get a bit harried. And then two dear friends, Joanne and Bruce Herb, gave me a subscription to the *Joyful Noiseletter*, published by the Fellowship of Merry Christians in Portage, Michigan. It is full of loving humor, and based on the premise that the scriptures contain more about rejoicing, about laughter, about joy, than about gloom and doom. It was just what I needed to keep my perspective. In working to achieve a healthy body, we are doing something that makes the angels rejoice. We not only ought to be happy about our efforts, we ought to leap with joy. For we are not doing this alone, but with the help of God, the help of friends, and the help of God's holy angels, who fight—and delight—with us.

When they came to the place that is called The Skull, they crucified Jesus there with the criminals, one on his right and one on his left. Then Jesus said, "Father, forgive them; for they do not know what they are doing."

—Luke 32:33-34a (NRSV)

❖

Forgiveness is an important issue when we are struggling to acquire a healthy body. Most of our failures are intimately tied to sin. Think about it. Do you pig out because you're angry at yourself for forgetting your father's birthday? Have you ever overeaten to the point of getting sick? Do you persist in eating stuff you're allergic to even though chocolate often gives you a migraine? All this is sin, either your own or others'. And we must deal with it, asking the forgiveness of a loving God, who loved us so much that he became one of us forever and ever. The good news is that he always forgives. He never holds our failures against us.

Bear with one another and, if anyone has a complaint against another, forgive each other; just as the Lord has forgiven you, so you also must forgive.

—Colossians 3:13 (NRSV)

❀

The other side of the forgiveness coin is granting forgiveness. We ask pardon of God, and of others when we have hurt them in any way at all. But we must also forgive all those who have ever hurt us. I remember when I went to my high school reunion years ago, I hoped that Mark, who had tormented me throughout my adolescence, would be there so I could embarrass him. I planned all sorts of revenge, I was still so wounded inside, even after all those years. By the mercy of God, he didn't come. But the wounds he had made in my spirit persisted until I consciously forgave him, as Christ has forgiven me, and released every burden, every obligation. I asked Christ to come into my heart and heal even the memories, and doing so freed me of a real obstacle to losing weight successfully.

In the same way, every good tree bears good fruit, but the bad tree bears bad fruit. A good tree cannot bear bad fruit, nor can a bad tree bear good fruit.

—Matthew 7:17-18 (NRSV)

❦

The good fruit of any weight loss program is actual weight loss. Like many people, when I began my program, I was forever on the scale looking for more lost ounces. And it was a source of anxiety to me. I was much happier when I checked my progress only every other day or less frequently. But actually getting on the scale can help keep us honest and living in reality. It's all too easy to "forget" just how many calories a handful of chips contains. I went through a period when I wasn't very careful—and I just couldn't bring myself to get on the scale. I knew I was putting too many of the wrong kinds of "fruits" in my mouth. Getting on the scale, seeing I'd gained a couple of pounds, was what I needed to tell God I was sorry, and to thank him for the help I knew he was giving me to succeed.

*I do not call you servants any longer,
because the servant does not know
what the master is doing; but I have called you
friends, because I have made known to you
everything that I have heard from my Father.*

—John 15:15 (NRSV)

❦

I used to beg God to help me on my diet. And then one day while I
was pleading and begging and (to state it frankly!) groveling before God,
the Lord told me point-blank, "Stop this begging and whining, dear heart!
Never beg me for anything. Would a loving God make his children beggars?
Ask me for everything you need, ask fervently, enthusiastically, but do it
confidently. I love you, and all you need is already yours in me." So I
changed my attitude and stopped using the word "beg." Instead, I ask,
and I am learning to trust that the ear of God is always listening.
Jesus is my friend, not a taskmaster.

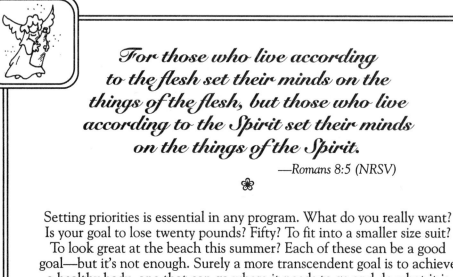

*For those who live according
to the flesh set their minds on the
things of the flesh, but those who live
according to the Spirit set their minds
on the things of the Spirit.*

—Romans 8:5 (NRSV)

❃

Setting priorities is essential in any program. What do you really want?
Is your goal to lose twenty pounds? Fifty? To fit into a smaller size suit?
To look great at the beach this summer? Each of these can be a good
goal—but it's not enough. Surely a more transcendent goal is to achieve
a healthy body, one that can go where it needs to go and do what it is
supposed to do. I found that to set proper goals, I needed a great deal of
prayer and a great deal of guidance from the Holy Spirit. Try to keep your
mind off food and onto higher things—even if the higher things have
to do with washing the car or pruning trees. God will do the rest.

And in the case of an athlete,
no one is crowned without
competing according to the rules.

—2 Timothy 2:5 (NRSV)

❀

Dieting has its rules, just as everything else does. And if we want to win, we must compete according to the rules. We've all read stories of athletes who thought they could cheat and win. It doesn't work that way. The basic rule of dieting is the one that we tell ourselves can't be all that simple: eat fewer calories than your body burns. And the corollary is: do whatever will make your body burn more calories. I have not described in this book my own weight loss program. It's not because I have a magic secret. I don't. But each person is an individual, and so each program must be tailored individually. My diet, which includes two days a week of fasting and prayer, is designed to help me listen to God and what God says to and within my body. But however exotic or plain your diet, you must stick to it and compete according to its rules.

He . . . fed him with produce of the field; he nursed him with honey . . . with oil . . . curds from the herd, and milk from the flock, with fat of lambs and rams . . . together with the choicest wheat. . . . Jacob ate his fill; Jeshurun grew fat, and kicked. You grew fat, bloated, and gorged! He abandoned God who made him, scoffed at the Rock of his salvation.

—Deuteronomy 32:13-15 (NRSV)

❀

When one is very fat, as I was, it is easy to forget God. Food becomes a god. It becomes a drug that causes us to forget God and who we are and what we supposed to be doing. There is nothing to do if this happens to us except to repent of it, to remember God again, and never to forget who is the Rock that saves us.

Do not be like a horse or a mule,
without understanding, whose temper
must be curbed with bit and bridle, else it
will not stay near you.

—*Psalms 32:9 (NRSV)*

❀

When we begin our program of weight loss, we generally have a great deal of energy and goodwill and commitment. But it's inevitable that we come to a point when we want to give up. We want God to take over and do all the work for us, to give us a rest from choices. That's not going to happen. Our ability to make free choices is one of our glories as human beings, and God will not take it from us. No angel will interfere with our free choices. But God does not call us to be stubborn as mules, either. We are to use our free will in a rational manner and not become compulsive and controlling in how and what and when we eat. We need to take our blinders off if we want to succeed in listening to God.

I have set before you life and death, blessings and curses. Choose life so that you and your descendants may live, loving the Lord your God, obeying him, and holding fast to him; for that means life to you and length of days. . . .

—Deuteronomy 30:19-20 (NRSV)

❀

Whenever we choose a healthy body for ourselves, we are choosing life, and we have God's word that choosing life leads not just to continued existence, but to abundant life. That's our purpose in trying to lose weight, after all—to have life in all its richness and abundance. We must choose life in everything we do—life for ourself and loved ones, life for the unborn, life for our enemies so they can become our friends, life for the earth itself. Have a life-choosing heart, and your dieting will be easier.

Athletes exercise self-control in all things; they do it to receive a perishable wreath, but we an imperishable one. So I do not run aimlessly, nor do I box as though beating the air; but I punish my body and enslave it, so that after proclaiming to others I myself should not be disqualified.

—1 Corinthians 9:25-27 (NRSV)

❁

Losing weight involves sticking to a program, whatever that is for you. It means setting voluntary limits on your food and food-related behaviors. It means exercising self-control. I have found that putting structure in my life helps me keep to a reasonable eating regimen, and eating only what I need when I need it helps me in many other ways apart from food. Think of your goals, as Paul did, and your aims, and achieve them.

> *"Come to me, all you that are weary*
> *and are carrying heavy burdens,*
> *and I will give you rest."*
>
> —Matthew 11:28 (NRSV)

❀

I've always taken this passage in two ways, the literal and the spiritual. Overweight is a heavy burden. It stresses every physical system we have, from our bones and joints to our blood pressure. But the greater burden is the guilt we carry as a result of our overindulgent lifestyle. Sometimes we feel so unlovable, because we look at our bodies and really hate ourselves. But Jesus loves us unconditionally. He never told us to make ourselves perfect and then come and follow him. In fact, he said specifically that he had come to call sinners—which we all are. He calls you to come to him and to release into his hands every burden, including your struggles with weight, and to enter into his rest. I have experienced the truth of this scripture. If you give him your burden, *he will take it from you.*

> *"Stolen water is sweet,*
> *and bread eaten in secret is pleasant."*
>
> —Proverbs 9:17 (NRSV)

❦

This text is in quotes because the speaker is a foolish woman trying to trap others in her folly. She sits outside the door, calling to the unwary to come in and taste of her food. The scripture goes on to say that whoever enters discovers that her house is filled with the dead! How many times have we sneaked food in secret? Be honest. If you're like me, you can't count the times. When we're at a party or a reception, we slip a few cookies in our pockets "for tomorrow." We hide food in our drawers or in the glove compartment of the car. We have all sorts of excuses for why we do it. And it's true that at the moment we eat our hidden dainties, they taste delicious. But the next morning when we realize we ate the whole package of candy or crackers or whatever, we feel terrible, like the unwary who enter the foolish woman's house. Isn't it much easier and much more peaceful not to hide food or sneak it in secret in the first place? God prefers that everything be out in the open.

If you have found honey, eat only enough for you, or else, having too much, you will vomit it. . . . It is not good to eat much honey, or to seek honor on top of honor.

—Proverbs 25:16, 27 (NRSV)

❀

This passage reminds us that even in the days when it was written, people knew that eating too many sweet things was not good. Today we know scientifically about the dangers of high blood sugar, of vitamin depletion, and so forth that can be caused by too much sugar. Some studies say that even using noncaloric sweeteners is of little help in dieting, because it never breaks us of the habit of wanting sweet things. Try going for a week without eating anything that contains any form of sweetener, nutritive or not. Read your labels carefully. If you can follow this plan, at the end of the week you'll be amazed at how your taste buds now react to the smallest bit of sugar, in fruit, in grains, even in vegetables. You'll need less of anything sweet to be satisfied.

Like a city breached, without walls,
is one who lacks self-control.
—Proverbs 25:28 (NRSV)

✸

Self-control is the key to a healthy weight, as we all know. And I have found that the only way to achieve self-control is to ask God for it. God will surely grant us this request. At one time, I was so much a prey to food that if I saw something in the supermarket that I wanted to eat, I simply bought and ate it—no reflection, no thinking, no weighing of choices. I just reached out and grabbed it. Sometimes I ate it before I even left the market, and gave the cashier an empty package to ring up. In ancient days, cities were surrounded by walls to prevent the entry of unauthorized people or armies. When we lack self-control, we are like a city whose walls have been broken down—vulnerable to attack. If you have trouble with self-control, try putting some imaginary walls around you before you go into danger areas like markets, parties, malls, whatever. Think of the fortified city that, with God's help, you are. God will give you victory, if you just ask for it and act out of that belief.

Thanks be to God, who gives us the victory through our Lord Jesus Christ.

—1 Corinthians 15:57 (NRSV)

❧

Losing weight and keeping it off is not about fighting a defensive war. It's about taking the offensive against a host of enemies, both physical and spiritual, and defeating them by the power of God and our faith in God's almighty power to transform our lives. We were never meant to be stuck in a holding pattern, or to hold a powerful enemy at bay. We are meant to be victorious, to gain mastery over our appetites, to see our wounds of spirit healed, our angers released, our peace restored. God intends for us to live life abundantly, not just to squeak through. The key to living in this victory is to give thanks always to God. Give thanks when you win a battle with God's help. Give thanks whenever you learn something about yourself and why, perhaps you listened to the voice that urged you to eat. Give thanks even if you falter, thanks that God is still there and his love has not changed, nor will it ever be turned away from you. God intends you to be victorious. Grasp it and give thanks!

Angelic
Affirmations

Affirmations are positive statements that help us focus our minds in directions we want to go. The practice of using affirmations is an ancient one, but most of us have heard them all our lives. Remember the old saying: "Every day in every way, I am getting better and better"? For me, the best affirmations remind us of sacred truths that transcend our own petty concerns. An affirmation like the above one is a very selfish affirmation. I prefer something more universal, that ties us in to God and to the Body of Christ, like: "As I continue to lose weight, God blesses me and those whose lives I touch." I suggest you find an affirmation that feels "right" for you, then repeat it slowly three times at least three times a day for a week.

*If I am not for myself, who
is for me? If I am only for myself,
what am I? If not now, when?*

❀

This ancient Jewish saying is one of my favorites. I have a wonderful
version in Hebrew calligraphy that for years hung above my corporate
desk. Now it hangs in my bedroom so I can remind myself that some
priorities never change. I must be concerned with myself, because in
the eyes of God I am worth it. I must be concerned for others, because I
am intimately involved with creation. And I must do it now,
because the Now is all we have.

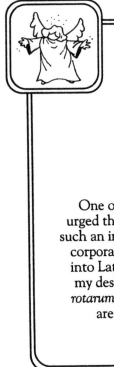

I will take it easy today.
I refuse to let myself be
overburdened with stress.

❀

One of my favorite songs growing up was "Take It Easy." The lyrics urged that we not let the sound of our own wheels drive us crazy. It was such an important affirmation for me later on, when my own job tour into corporate life had become hairy, that I took the lyrics, translated them into Latin (so no one would know what they said!) and hung them by my desk. For those similarly minded, they run: *Noli permittere sonitum rotarum tuarum te reddere insanem.* The point is that tension and stress are states of mind in which it's all too easy to forget our plans and to eat inappropriately.

*I can do all things in Christ
who gives me my strength.*

✿

This paraphrase of the scriptures is one of my favorite affirmations.
I use it not so much as an everyday affirmation, but in special situations.
When I try to keep my calories within bounds at a party, for example, I
use this affirmation to remind myself that with God's help I can eat
appropriately. Getting through a party or a picnic or a barbeque
without overeating can be tough, but knowing that Christ and
his angels are standing with me is a great help.

*My body is growing in health
every day as I eat only healthful
foods in the amounts I need.*

❀

Try to develop an affirmation that states concisely what your food goals
for the day are. It shouldn't be a long catalog, just a brief reminder. The
one on this page is just a sample. You might want to create something
special for unusual circumstances. For example: While I am on vacation,
I remain with my regular program, because I choose to continue losing
weight at this time. Or: At the dinner party tonight I will choose from
foods that I can eat, avoiding the others, because I intend to
maintain my health and my weight loss.

Angel of God, my guardian dear,
To whom God's love entrusts me here,
Ever this day be at my side,
To lead and guard, to light and guide.

❀

This is really more of a prayer than an affirmation, but I use it as an affirmation, because it reminds me that angels are watching me, not as judges, but as caring fellow travelers, whom God has appointed to help me draw near to him. It comes out of the Roman Catholic religious tradition but is now used much more widely. I don't believe angels are fairy godmothers who will wave magic wands over us and take the calories out of our ice cream. But I do believe they are messengers from God who are sent to remind us of God's ever-present help, and to help us to turn to the loving Creator who wants us to become perfect in every way.

God loves me unconditionally,
and therefore I love myself just as I am.

❀

Oh, the trauma of looking at ourselves naked in a mirror, seeing every flaw, every physical imperfection! It can be a real killer, especially if our self-image has been damage by years of failure to lose weight and keep it off. How many times have we wounded ourselves by saying, usually through clenched teeth, "I hate how I look! I hate myself for eating that bag of cookies!" And then we assume that God is the same way, and because we hate ourselves, surely God must hate us, too. Nothing could be further from the truth. God is love, and God created us out of love. And God never changes. Love isn't something God does when it suits. God is love. To live in God's plan we must love ourselves as totally and unconditionally as God loves us.

*I am secure in loving myself,
and therefore I love others as myself.*

❀

For me, the hardest, and yet the most necessary part of losing weight and keeping it off was to believe that I am lovable. For so many years I hated myself, and I lived without joy. Jesus once said that the first and the greatest commandment is to love God with all our heart, our soul, our strength. He also said that the second commandment was like the first: to love our neighbors as ourselves. But if we don't love ourselves to begin with, how can we love others with a real, positive, transforming love? If you have been seriously overweight all your life, your self-love may also be in serious need of healing. Pray more than anything for the Spirit of God to help you understand how much God loves you, and then live your life believing it. Like any affirmation, this may take a while to sink in, but God will use it as a means of sending his love into your heart.

*I entrust my entire day to God,
knowing that a loving Spirit watches
over me to help me, and that uncounted angels
and saints are praying for me to succeed.*

❀

Surrender to God's loving plan for my life is a major part of my philosophy.
I don't believe God is jerking my strings and telling me when to breathe
and whether to buy a pair of socks, but I do believe that there is a plan,
and that I fit into that plan, and that there are things that only I can do.
And if I am not healthy and reasonably fit, I cannot do them and part of
the plan will remain forever unfulfilled. So I seek to know and be part of
that plan, and I remind myself of this frequently. I also remind myself that
I am not alone. I have an immense cheering section made up of angels and
all those who are a part of the "great cloud of witnesses" of which
Hebrews 12:1 speaks. It is comforting and calls me to account.

I sign myself with the sign of the cross, and I cover myself with the blood of the Lamb, and I draw around myself a circle of light, which represents the protection of Almighty God, and I say in the name of Jesus Christ that nothing shall get through it to hurt me. Amen.

❋

This is an affirmation used by Agnes Sanford, a devout Christian pioneer in the healing ministry in the Church for most of this century. The wife of an Episcopal priest and mother of three, she believed that Jesus spoke for us today when he said that in his name believers would do not only the works he did but even greater ones. Her affirmation reminds us that the power of Christ, who is the light of the world, to protect and heal us is rooted in Calvary. I use this affirmation daily, particularly in times of great testing, and as I visualize the cross, it's amazing how quickly my oft-skewed perspectives on life are refocused. *Amen* means "So be it. I believe."

*I will succeed in losing weight
and keeping it off because I know
God is helping me.*

❀

Whenever we think or speak words like *diet, program, plan, maintenance, exercise, training,* we should breathe the word *God.* God is the source, the fuel, the material, the inspiration, the beginning and the end of everything we do to achieve a healthy weight. Jesus said, "I am the Alpha and the Omega, the Beginning and the End." The minute we try to make something else the real end or goal is the minute when we set ourselves up for some nasty surprises. But if we keep affirming that God is our strength, we will have enough energy to do everything we need to do—not just in the area of weight loss, but in everything.

*The light of God is reaching deep
into all the wounded parts of my life
and healing the hurt memories in my past. I
choose to forgive all those who have ever hurt me.*

❀

We often eat to forget old wounds and to comfort ourselves when we are
depressed or stressed or when others have hurt us. As strange as this may
seem to you, deciding by an act of will to forgive those who have hurt you
is one of the most critical steps you can take toward victory over poor
eating habits. The more you can ask Jesus to come into your heart and
heal the wounded memories of the past, the more easily you will lose
weight and learn new, more healthy ways of nourishing your body. I
earnestly recommend Agnes Sanford's book, *The Healing Light*, which
speaks to many issues concerning the healing of our memories and how
and why we must forgive if we want to be healed ourselves.

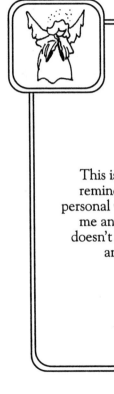

I am in the presence of God.

❀

This is the simplest of affirmations, and I use it many times a day to remind myself that I am never alone, that a loving, caring, merciful, personal God who knows and helps and guides and forgives is always with me and is, in fact, closer to me than my heartbeat and my breath. It doesn't help me to lose weight, but it does help me to love and to trust and to build a climate that is the absolute antithesis of fear.

As I continue to lose weight, God blesses me and all those whose lives I touch.

❀

God wants us to be healthy. Therefore, it is God's design, God's will, that we weigh what is appropriate for us so that we can do with joy and ease all the good works that God has appointed for us to walk in. Dieting can be a struggle that exhausts us and makes us depressed, or it can be a joyful walk with God that refreshes us in ways that go far beyond the material. I know this for a fact, because I have experienced it: no matter how hard the effort is, the blessings that God showers on those who live according to the divine plan are many, and they more than compensate for the grunt work we undertake when we are dieting or exercising.

*I choose what foods I put
in my mouth, listening only to the
Spirit and to what I know to be true.*

❀

Sometimes we need to stand firm against our friends, family, and
co-workers who have their own agendas for us. Those we know may
actually try to sabotage our efforts, because our increasing freedom is
threatening to them. As we lose weight, it reminds them that they can't
quit smoking, or that they may drink too much, or gamble their
paychecks, or whatever. So they may try to force another cookie on us or a
second helping of pot roast. We need to affirm that *we* decide, *we* choose
what we will eat, and no one else. We affirm that we listen to the guidance
of the Holy Spirit, who may speak to us through our angels or not, and
we also listen to sound medical advice, which is a necessary part
of any weight-loss program.

Blessings
and
Prayers

Giving thanks to God is one of the basic forms of prayer. As St. Paul says to the Thessalonians, "Give thanks in all circumstances; for this is the will of God in Christ Jesus for you." I believe that when we enter into a weight reduction program, our prayers of praise and thanksgiving should equal or even outweigh our petitions to God to help us succeed. St. Paul says that nothing should be rejected out of hand if we can give thanks for it. We may not be able to eat very much chocolate ice cream or lasagna, because they are high in calories, but we should be able to give thanks for a small serving. All things come from God, as Psalm 50 reminds us: "For every wild animal of the forest is mine, the cattle on a thousand hills." Give thanks for every bit of food you eat and every bit you decide not to eat. Remember that one day, in God's plan, you will be able to eat it again.

Blessing of Bread

*Blessed are you, O God, Creator
of all things, who bring forth bread from the
earth, and who fed our ancestors with heavenly
bread in the wilderness. May this bread of earth
strengthen my body and unite me to my sisters
and brothers everywhere.*

❀

Bread is such a basic food that we often forget its significance. Bread is made up of many grains leavened and raised together. It is a metaphor for our life. Whenever I eat bread, I first break it in half and kiss it; then I use this blessing to give thanks.

Blessing of Wine

***Blessed are you, O Lord our God,
King of the universe, who have created
the fruit of the vine.***

❧

Jewish tradition has always offered a blessing for wine. Although
many people cannot or choose not to drink alcoholic beverages, such
beverages are no more inherently evil than bread. For those who
can receive it with thanks, wine is indeed, as the scriptures say,
a drink to gladden the human heart (Judges 9:13).

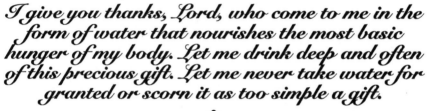

Blessing of Water

I give you thanks, Lord, who come to me in the form of water that nourishes the most basic hunger of my body. Let me drink deep and often of this precious gift. Let me never take water for granted or scorn it as too simple a gift.

❀

All the books remind us that when we think we're hungry, most often we're actually thirsty. At such moments, what we need is a good glass of water. We can, in dire emergencies, be cut off from food for months and still survive, but without water we die in days. Drink lots of water every day, and give thanks for each glass you drink. Millions of people all over the world have no safe drinking water. And as you drink and give thanks, consider what you might do to help them.

Breakfast Blessing

Dear God, I ask you to bless this first meal of the rest of my life. Let it nourish my body and help me achieve good health. At 10:00 this morning, when I crave a doughnut at work, let me remember that you have already nourished me for the morning, and let me draw my food from your love.

❁

Breakfast can be an important meal of the day, but it's easy to forget we've eaten it. If our breakfast includes enough protein and complex carbohydrates and is not top-heavy with fat and empty calories, it will sustain us easily until lunchtime and well beyond.

Prayer for Strength to Choose

Please give me strength, Lord, to pass on the pretzels and to choose the carrot sticks today. Give me also the strength to love them equally, even if right now I choose not to eat them equally. Give me strength to see in my heart the day when I'll be able to choose to eat those pretzels again. Thank you for your strength. I can't do it by myself.

❀

If we trust God for the strength we need, we will succeed. God is stronger than any need we will ever have; there is no limit to God's power and will to help us. Therefore we are unlimited in our ability to succeed.

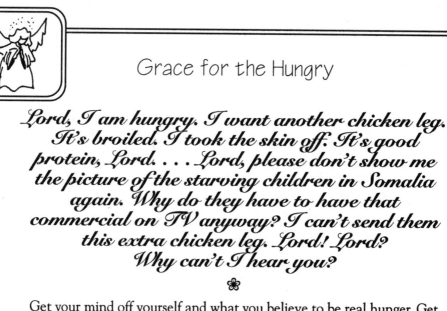

Grace for the Hungry

Lord, I am hungry. I want another chicken leg. It's broiled. I took the skin off. It's good protein, Lord. . . . Lord, please don't show me the picture of the starving children in Somalia again. Why do they have to have that commercial on TV anyway? I can't send them this extra chicken leg. Lord! Lord? Why can't I hear you?

❁

Get your mind off yourself and what you believe to be real hunger. Get involved in helping those who know real want in this world. Bring food to a local pantry or help out there yourself. Get a better perspective.

Blessing for Brunch

Well, I got up late this morning, dear God. It's after eleven. I guess I missed breakfast. Of course, I could combine lunch and breakfast calories and have a really big brunch. After all, why shouldn't I treat myself? It's not like I'm going to eat more total calories than I should!

❀

This is a dangerous grace for anyone, because it borders on giving up the virtue of self-control. My mother always said, "Leave the table a little hungry." I never followed her advice, but it's good advice. Don't eat anything just because you can; eat what you need when you need it. If you get up late and want scrambled eggs, maybe that's all right. But to have both eggs and a cheese sandwich because you can is a bad idea.

A Snacker's Prayer

Please give me the grace to eat one apple, or maybe this big red pepper, or just a few fat-free crackers with a little hummus, or maybe this one big cucumber in diet dressing, with a diet cola, of course, and just one cookie, Lord, together with those little carrot pieces. . . .

❁

Snacking is a hard problem to lick, so to speak. It's so easy to deceive ourselves about the calorie content of what we eat on the fly. We need to ask whether we need a particular food before we give thanks for it and put it in our mouths. The good news is that, if we listen, God will answer.

A Midnight Snacker's Prayer

Dear God, I've heard that it's OK to snack at night, because the calories can't see in the dark to get into the food. Maybe if I don't turn the light on, the calories will just go away. What do you think? Do you do that? No, I didn't really think you did. I had a good dinner, so I can't be hungry. What's really going on inside that I'm trying to make food a substitute for?

❀

If you are tempted to eat at unusual hours, try to understand why. Was there an earlier disappointment, a frustration, anger? Did you need comfort? Find out why before you snack—and you may not need to.

A Repentant Snacker's Prayer

I blew it, God! I said I'd only have a dozen fat-free potato chips, and I ate the whole bag before I knew it. I'm sorry. Oh, I'm so awful, I hate myself. I'm a total failure. I'll never . . .

❀

"Hold on there, dear heart," says the Lord. "I know you made a mistake in judgment, but that doesn't change My love for you. Nothing can change that. I accept your apology. Let's forget it, shall we? Just remember to subtract the number of extra calories from what you have left for today."

Grace before Lunch

Well, Lord, it's noon, and time for lunch. Thank you for this food. Help me to take the time to relax and enjoy it. May it nourish my body, so that you can care for my spirit. Let me feed on the blessings of this day while I eat, and return refreshed to my work.

❀

When we are in a rush, we eat faster, and generally we eat more than we had planned, unless we bring our food with us in a specific amount and no more. But there are other reasons to eat slowly. We digest food better, and it puts less stress on our systems. If we eat too much and too fast, with too much anxiety, our spirits can be burdened as well as our bodies, and we go back to our tasks tired. So slow down.

A Dinner Blessing

Lord, why do I find dinner the toughest meal of the day? Is it because I've been cooking for the past hour and the casserole smells great? Is it because the food will be sitting right in front of me? Is it because those who share the table with me can eat all they want and I've chosen not to? Please help me to eat moderately, and to take some of my nourishment from the conversation, not just from the food.

❋

If it's dinner hour, know that I'm praying for you to win.

Thanks for Many Pasta-bilities

Are you Italian at heart, God, or maybe I should say Chinese, since they seem to have invented pasta to begin with? Thank you for such a wonderful food that comes in so many shapes and flavors. Please help me to find things to put on it that will help me keep to my program, so that one day I'll be more of an angel-hair pasta than a rigatoni!

❀

Pasta is surprisingly low in calories. It's the alfredo sauce, the butter, the heaps of parmesan, the meat sauce, or the mayonnaise that makes a hot or cold pasta dish a problem. Be creative with veggies and herbs, and enjoy!

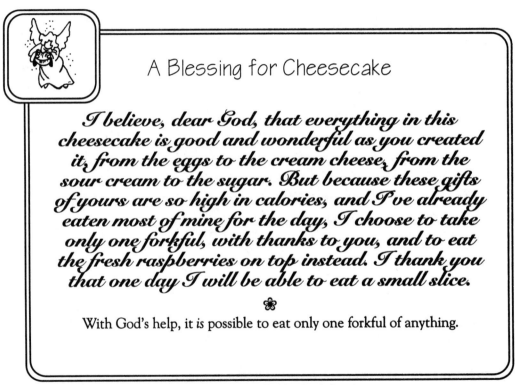

A Blessing for Cheesecake

I believe, dear God, that everything in this cheesecake is good and wonderful as you created it, from the eggs to the cream cheese, from the sour cream to the sugar. But because these gifts of yours are so high in calories, and I've already eaten most of mine for the day, I choose to take only one forkful, with thanks to you, and to eat the fresh raspberries on top instead. I thank you that one day I will be able to eat a small slice.

❀

With God's help, it *is* possible to eat only one forkful of anything.

A Chocoholic's Prayer

Dear God, do I love you more than this delectable morsel of dark chocolate filled with strawberry ganache and dusted with only the finest Belgian cocoa? Can I pass up this chance to sink my teeth into this apex of the chocolatier's art? It's only 500 calories and 35 grams of fat. . . .

❀

How many times do we stand in front of something that calls to us that we know we can't possibly choose to eat and still eat responsibly? But do we really think before we eat, or do we let our taste buds rule our reason? Pray before you eat anything that's not on your "A" list. God will send an angel to open your heart and mind to the answer.

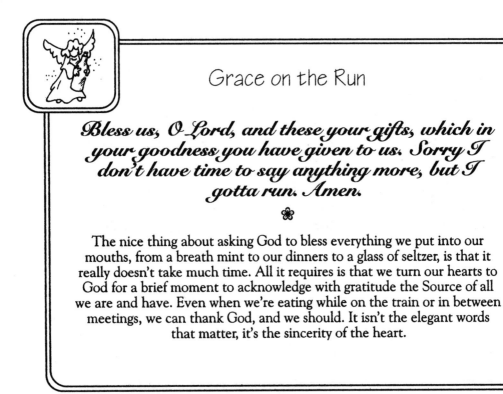

Grace on the Run

Bless us, O Lord, and these your gifts, which in your goodness you have given to us. Sorry I don't have time to say anything more, but I gotta run. Amen.

❀

The nice thing about asking God to bless everything we put into our mouths, from a breath mint to our dinners to a glass of seltzer, is that it really doesn't take much time. All it requires is that we turn our hearts to God for a brief moment to acknowledge with gratitude the Source of all we are and have. Even when we're eating while on the train or in between meetings, we can thank God, and we should. It isn't the elegant words that matter, it's the sincerity of the heart.

Prayer of Thanksgiving

God, thank you so much for helping me tonight. Everything looked so good, and I really wanted that second helping of spaghetti, and it was so hard to pass up the garlic bread and the spumoni and to choose some seltzer instead of the wine. I didn't think I could say No, but I did—with your help. Thank you, really, God, thanks!

❀

The sensation of victory we experience when we defeat the urge to eat inappropriately is wonderful, because it makes us realize the truth of the scripture that Christ has set us free to be free, and that we do not ever need to live in slavery to anything. Remember every small victory, treasure them, and remember them when things get tough.

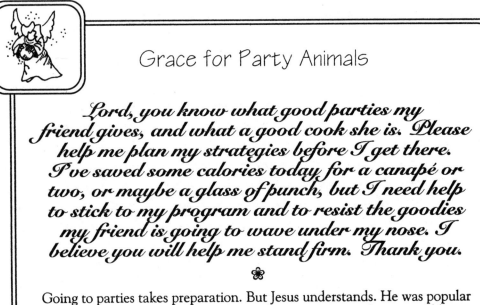

Grace for Party Animals

Lord, you know what good parties my friend gives, and what a good cook she is. Please help me plan my strategies before I get there. I've saved some calories today for a canapé or two, or maybe a glass of punch, but I need help to stick to my program and to resist the goodies my friend is going to wave under my nose. I believe you will help me stand firm. Thank you.

❀

Going to parties takes preparation. But Jesus understands. He was popular at parties, especially after he changed water into wine for one wedding couple. Ask him to give you special wisdom and insight, and he will.

I Love Food!

God, I love food! I don't think I really hate anything except maybe guacamole and smelly cheeses. Thank you for creating so many kinds of food. I want to try everything—and one day I will, in moderation. But for today, I choose to pass up certain foods because I have a more wonderful goal in mind.

❀

There's nothing wrong with loving food. It's not an enemy. God has given it to us as a gift of love. Thousands of kinds of plants are edible, but most of us eat barely a hundred. I even like to eat wild foods like daylilies and ferns. All food is good, but when we're on a program to reduce our weight, we must learn to make intelligent choices.

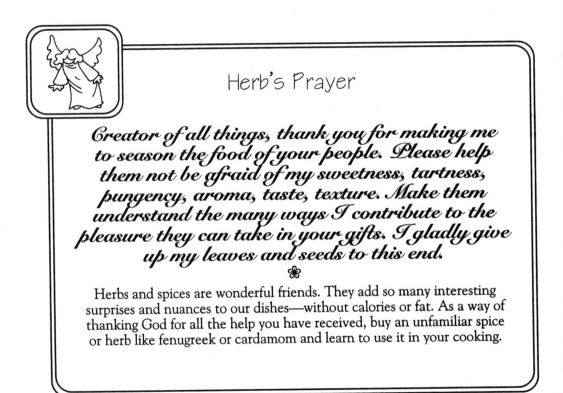

Herb's Prayer

Creator of all things, thank you for making me to season the food of your people. Please help them not be afraid of my sweetness, tartness, pungency, aroma, taste, texture. Make them understand the many ways I contribute to the pleasure they can take in your gifts. I gladly give up my leaves and seeds to this end.

❀

Herbs and spices are wonderful friends. They add so many interesting surprises and nuances to our dishes—without calories or fat. As a way of thanking God for all the help you have received, buy an unfamiliar spice or herb like fenugreek or cardamom and learn to use it in your cooking.

Restaurant Grace

Well, dear God, here I am with a menu six miles long and everything on it covered in cream sauce. What am I supposed to do now? I've been so good all day. I don't want to blow it. I didn't even want to come to this place. I'm afraid. Help!

❄

Restaurants can be tough, even though most of them have a dish or two that is low in fat and calories. It's the extras—the rolls and butter, the free cheese and crackers, the Chinese noodles and sauce—that do us in. Don't panic. God's grace is enough to help you steer a safe course between the fried clams and the chiles rellenos. Ask God to take away your fear, take a deep breath, and then look at the menu as if it were a science book—with your mind. Ask the waiter for help. Trust that God will provide.

Perseverance

Lord, it's so hard to keep on going. I've reached a plateau, and for the past week I haven't lost an ounce, and I still have 40 pounds to lose! The end is nowhere in sight, and I'm tired and hungry. Give me the strength to persevere, knowing that you are with me, and that you were once hungry in the wilderness.

❦

Sometimes, for all our trust, it's hard not to let a note of grumpiness seep into our prayers. It's all right, dear heart. God understands. God never holds our moods against us. When God walked the earth, he was hungry. I'm sure his travels kept him on the lean side, but he knew hunger. He won't let you down. Strength is there. Reach out for it.

The First Day

Thank you for the grace to start this diet, dear God. I know it won't always be easy, but I believe that with you all things are possible, and I know you will help me at every moment, and your angels will whisper your good word in my ear. I trust in you and not myself for strength, and I am confident that together we will succeed.

Congratulations on beginning your program, whatever it is to be. I know how hard it is, and God knows far, far better than I. I prayed for you today, dear sister or brother, and I ask God to give you joy and courage as you start on this great adventure in love and health and self-control. Lean on God for courage, and ask him to send your angel to help, and you will win.

Goal!

*I don't believe the scale! It really says
I've reached my goal. Thank you, thank you,
dear God, for helping me all along the way. I
could never have done it without your grace.
I'm so happy I could dance. I think I will!*

❀

Whether our goal is 20 pounds or 200, a smaller size or the ability to walk
a mile without keeling over, the moment we reach it is bound to be an
emotional one. We deserve to rejoice, to laugh, to sing, to dance. I never
could dance, because I didn't have the endurance, and because I was
wounded by humiliating moments I endured as a teenager. But God
healed me of all that as I lost weight, and now I enjoy contra dancing. I'm
not a great dancer, but I'm having fun I never could have had before.

The Day After Goal

I reached my goal yesterday, God, and I still want to dance. But what do I do now? How do I keep off the weight? How do I tone up my flab? Guide me now more than ever—please!

❀

"Of course I am here to help you, dear heart," says the Lord. "I love you. And I am so proud of you; I'm the one who is dancing, and all my angels with me. Don't be afraid. I will guide you in peace and in victory, because you are infinitely precious in my sight. Trust me and know that if you listen to me, I will continue to guide you by my Spirit and show you how to continue to eat in joy, in confidence, and with care. We did it!"

EILEEN ELIAS FREEMAN directs the activities of The AngelWatch™ Foundation, Inc. and also publishes the *AngelWatch™ Journal*, a bimonthly periodical about angels. She is the author of the bestselling books *Touched by Angels*, *The Angels' Little Instruction Book*, *Angelic Healing*, and *Mary's Little Instruction Book*. Ms. Freeman holds a master's degree in theology from the University of Notre Dame and a B.A. in comparative religion from Barnard College. For information about AngelWatch, or to request information about Ms. Freeman's talks and workshops on angels, prayer, diet, spirituality, and related subjects, please send a long, stamped (or enclose two I.R.C.s for overseas mail), self-addressed envelope to The AngelWatch Foundation, P.O. Box 1397, Mountainside, NJ 07092.